BEYOND FEARS

A Practical Information Guide on How to Live, Work and Do Business in Nigeria.

An Insight on Facts, Fears, Myths and Opportunities.

Joel O. Akande

Fertility Specialist and Gynaecologist
Medico-Legal and Business Consultant.
Founder and Chief Executive Officer at
STRATEGIC INSIGHT HEALTHCARE
Lagos, Nigeria

Galaxy Books: Unit of Strategic Insight Publishing (SIP)
Part of Strategic Insight

©All rights reserved. © Joel Akande. April 2019.
© Cover and Internal designs by Strategic Insight Publishing

No part of this book may be reproduced, stored in a retrieval system, or be transmitted by any means without the written permission of the author and or the publisher.

The facts and or opinions expressed in this book are entirely the personal views and the legal responsibility of the author.

First published by Strategic Insight Publishing
ISBN 13:978-1-908064-35-6

British Library Cataloguing in Publication Data
A record for this book is available from the British Library

TABLE OF CONTENTS

Acknowledgement: 5

Dedication: 6

Introduction: 9

Chapter 1: Background - 15
Geography, Demography, History, Legal Systems, Politics, Culture and Economy of Nigeria.

Chapter 2: Infrastructure - The Nigerian Plague - 37
Failures in Legal, Transport, Healthcare, Housing, Water Systems. Communication, Energy /Power Supply, Education, Security, Commerce Including Official Registry, Financial and Credit Systems.

Chapter 3: Nigeria's Business Climate - 71
The Peculiarity of Nigeria. Incredible and Untapped Opportunities: Potential Power House. Factors Limiting Growth. Regulatory Framework and Business Forms.

Chapter 4: Cautions, Pitfalls and Warnings - 105
Trust, Utilities, Will and Trust for Legacy Preservation, Personal Requirements, Material Requirements for An Aspiring Nigerian Resident.

Appendix of Key Official Services (Federal and Lagos State): 118

References: 125

Other Books by the Same Author: 126

Beyond Fears

Acknowledgement.

I wish to acknowledge the contribution of my friend and editor: Rhoda Sawa. She simplified my masculine aggressive language and made the book more readable. That said, I take responsibility for all and any error that may be in this book.

Further, as a writer, I value the intellectuality and proprietary ownership of artists and innovators. If for any reason I have failed to acknowledge and or credit any source of information that is in this book, I certainly did not do so deliberately. I hope to be forgiven for any omission.

Dedication

To everyone who in the face of severe opposition, persevere to overcome prevailing challenges in order to add value to their community and to their fellow human beings.

Nigeria:

A beautiful rose flower with a manifold of thorns attached.

Beyond Fears

Beyond Fears

Introduction
"Let me win, but if I cannot win, let me be brave in the attempt."
- Motto of the Special Olympics

When I moved to live in Nigeria in 2011, my friends were very concerned. They wondered if I had thought this decision through properly, as a sudden decision to relocate to Nigeria from United Kingdom appeared outlandish. My mind was not only sound but I was also fit as a fiddle. Some even wondered if I had been deported from the United Kingdom. Their thoughts and suspicions were silenced when they noticed how often and easily I travelled to and from the United Kingdom.

From the time of my departure from the United Kingdom up until the time of my writing this book, a countless number of people in Nigeria and in the Western hemisphere have asked me why I had to leave the comfort and conveniences of Britain to live in the harsh realities of Nigeria considering the fact that many Nigerians are so desirous of relocating to Europe and America which I had left. They dreamed of being in my shoes. My relocation in their own thinking just didn't make sense and had left them perplexed and confused.

In the course of providing explanations and reassurances to these inquirers, I have practically become a Counsellor, an Immigration expert, a Business consultant and a Motivator.

Though a Briton by immigration rights, I was born, bred and educated in Nigeria up to my first university degree. I had worked in Nigeria before I immigrated to Europe. Having had the opportunity to return to Nigeria, I could now reflect on both worlds that I belonged to and considered as home to me. I could see the strengths and weaknesses in both Nigerian and European lifestyles. I could also see and appreciate the opportunities and risks of life in both societies.

Since my return in 2011, I have gained a wider perspective on life and with this more matured mindset, I have been able to study Nigeria in more practical ways than before. So much so that I now run my own business in Nigeria. The opportunity of interacting with different communities, suppliers, employees, business clients/customers, friends, families, religious bodies and individuals, government officials amongst others have broadened my views extensively.

For these reasons, I have written this book to educate and enlighten others about Nigeria in general, and Lagos in particular. Lagos is the economic heartbeat of Nigeria and the 5th largest economy in Africa.

In respect of Nigeria, it's no secret that Nigeria by name and character has a negative connotation attached to it all over the world. Many Nigerians are ashamed of their country. Yet, for millions of Nigerians, there is nowhere else to call their home. Nigerians at home work hard and many ask of me, how to make their lives better. As a Physician, I see first-hand, the needless distress and diseases that Nigerians suffer from considering the size and wealth in resources available to Nigeria as a nation.

From my personal experience as a victim to injustice in Nigeria, my business was illegally shut down for ten days until I had paid a N250,000 fine to the State Government officials. On another occasion, local government officials threatened to demolish my building and close my business falsely purporting I owed and must pay N343,000. I fought these cases. It turned out the threats were all geared towards one thing: defrauding me of money. For one of the cases, I had to write a letter of complaint to the State Governor about the impunity and excesses of his civil servants. Yet, in another case, a neighbour who had some power in his hand as a junior civil servant, threatened to demolish my building unless I "cooperate." The term "to cooperate" means illegal financial payment to him.

An established resident in Nigeria is well aware of these manipulations. It will come as a rude shock to a would-be resident though. However, these are the experiences and many more, most especially perpetrated by persons who hold a position of trust and authority towards their fellow Nigerian citizens and residents. You will need to develop thick skin and determination not to run away in frustration. The value at stake is too high to be abandoned.

In truth, many Nigerian migrants scattered across all the nations of the earth, desire to return to Nigeria. One recurring theme that stands between them and their actual return is the dilemma that is wrapped up in the following inquiries: "What will I do when I get to Nigeria? How will I survive? How will I fit in? Where do I start from?" On the other hand, the fear of Nigeria is akin to religious fear of a leper or modern day panic about Ebola disease.

To further complicate the issue and reinforce these fears, a lot of Diaspora returnees have had to "run back" to where they came from: Europe, America and Asia because they discovered to their sadness, that they were unable to cope in Nigeria. In truth and in reality, such individuals are untutored and are unprepared for the life in Nigeria. Had they receive advanced counselling and or been fully prepared ahead of their return, the story may have been different.

Beyond Fears

Still, it's shocking to note that the people that seem to fear Nigeria most are Nigerians that were originally born in Nigeria. This generation, also instil the fear of the country on their offspring: "Don't go there", they say to their children.

In some ways, a highly traumatised individual whose injuries were effected in Nigeria and who had no justice but has a chance to escape from Nigeria as is sometimes the case, may swear never to return to the country. They are justified. However, it should be remembered, that the parents, siblings and families of emigrants may continue to live in Nigeria as are millions of compatriots that have no route to escaping the realities of the country.

On the other hand, I have seen Lebanese, Indians and other Asians, Britons, Europeans and Americans that have prospered in and made Nigeria their permanent home. In fact, it's commonly said in Nigeria that foreigners hardly ever want to leave Nigeria. The logic in the saying goes that, the level of individual freedom (I say occasioned by lawlessness) to do as one wishes is unmatched anywhere else. So, aliens can be anything and behave anyhow without legal accountability. Who would want to abandon such a level of individual freedom?

That said, the lure of opportunities to make money in Nigeria, in what some friends call "at ease" may be too much for some insightful businesses and individuals to resist. The thought goes that, one poor person may become a millionaire overnight in Nigeria. While that may be true for some, it's generally not the rule. Millions of Nigerians are actually hard workers. One thing is sure: if you are ignorant in Nigeria, not only are you vulnerable to exploitation, you may suffer unnecessarily. Readers should also be aware that, just as any country such as UK, France, USA and so forth, has a system by which it operates, in same manner, Nigeria has its own "system" no matter our opinion of this system. It's the failure to understand and to key into this "system" that often leads to (in what I call, all things being equal), failure of adaptation.

I want you the reader to note that I have gained valuable experience that I have distilled in this book. In the early 2000s shortly after the fear of "Millennium Bug" was over, I set up a business of recruitment in Nigeria. I was running the business from the UK with two offices in high brow business districts in Lagos State. I was visiting Nigeria about quarterly to oversee the business. The business failed because for one, I trusted Nigerians to share the vison but most importantly, I was in a long distance of over 3000miles but trying to manage a business. Each time I was around, the business will boom. Before I landed in Britain on return journey, the revenue would have disappeared and problems have mounted. You should never fall into the same mistake for many people still do.

For all of these, I have written this book to provide an insight into how to live, work and do business in Nigeria. I hope readers will view the book as a practical guide to enable them to fulfil their aspirations.

Beyond Fears

Chapter 1

Background
Geography, Demographics, History, Legal Systems, Politics, Culture and Economy of Nigeria

"If you build the guts to do something, anything, then you better save enough to face the consequences."
— *Criss Jami,*

I shall begin my narration with the background of Nigeria as a Nation. Somehow, you may have met a Nigerian or heard about Nigeria: for ill or for good. To a lot on people in the world and not just Nigerians, Nigeria is an enigma. Nigeria is a country that puzzles everyone. This is so, because of the importance of the county to the world considering the human and earthly resources that Nigeria is endowed with.

The purpose of this chapter is to draw your attention as a reader to the human, material and economic potentials of Nigeria as well as to reflect on the enormity of the diversity and the challenges that the country possesses. As you read further, you will become fully aware of some of the issues that are clearly responsible for the poor economic and human capital indices that are associated with Nigeria. To give you a clue to the intended terrain, an examination in summary of Nigeria's background will be necessary. To start with, Nigeria, for many reasons, is far too important to the world. The country cannot be ignored. You may also wish to know that Nigeria gained her independence from Britain on first of October, 1960.

The People: In brief, Nigeria as a Country has an area of 923,768 sq. km (356,669 sq. miles). The major languages are English (official), Yoruba, Ibo and Hausa. The total number of languages and dialects are over 250 in number. The dominant religions are Islam and Christianity with an estimated equal strength of 40% each. Practitioners of traditional religions and atheists make up the rest. I will further expatiate later on in the book, matters that relate to religion.

The Demographics:

Population
Data crunching may not be to the taste of everyone, but you need the data in order to fully understand the magnitude of the issues surrounding Nigeria especially as you weigh your options of living in Nigeria or not. Nigeria ranks amongst the top 10 most populated countries in the world. According to United Nations data as of 2018, Nigeria's population stands as 195,875,000. By another estimate, by February of 2019, Nigeria's population stood at about 198,924,841 according to World Population Review. This accounts place Nigeria as the 7th most populous country in the world. The population density is about 217/sq km and records a population growth rate of 2.6% annually. At the current rate, the current projections for 2050 are over 390 million total residents. It might interest you to know that the current estimated 51.9% of the population is urban (104,282,822 people in 2019) with median age of 17.9 years. The fertility rate as at February 2019 is 5.67% according to World Meters population figures. Most of the population is a young population, with 42.54% between the ages of 0–14. There is also a very high dependency ratio of the country at 88.2 dependents per 100 non-dependents according to Wikipedia data. The proportion of children under the age of 15 in 2010

was 44.0%. 53.2% was between 15 and 65 years of age, while 2.7% was 65 years or older. There are, according to estimates, about 1.04 males to every one female in the country. You should take note though that while women are slightly outnumbered by men; after the age of 65, the population of women outnumber men. The, life expectancy in Nigeria is, to put it mildly, pathetic: being unfortunately, the lowest in all of West Africa. The average life expectancy is around 54.5 years of age according to WHO data, with men living an average of 53.7 years and women living an average of 55.4 years.

These very low numbers of life expectancies can be attributed to the fact that the country has many health issues. In terms of access to clean drinking water, 68.5% of Nigerians have improved means of access while 31.5% still struggle to get clean water. Similarly, when examining access to sanitation facilities, only 29% of the entire populace of Nigeria has access to improved sanitation as compared to the 71% that are still struggling. The average number of years spent in school here in Nigeria is approximately 9 years, with national literacy rate at only 59.6%.

Health Indices: The above mentioned data is quite worrisome but still taking it a step further, Nigeria's health indices are a cause for genuine concern. Nigeria records a maternal mortality rate of 814 deaths per 100,000 women (WHO/World Bank/UNDP/UNICEF figures of 2015) and infants (children under one year old) mortality rate records about 69 deaths per 1000 live births in a given year. Nigeria has the 9th highest rankingof infant mortality rate in the world behind the likes of Somalia and Afghanistan. Every 10 minutes, one woman dies because of pregnancy or childbirth in Nigeria, giving 53,000 deaths per year. Nigeria's newborn death rate (neonatal mortality) is 528 per day making it one of the highest in the world. More than a quarter of the estimated 1 million children who die under the age of 5 years annually in Nigeria die during the first 28 days of life (neonatal period). I should also point out that about 9 out of 10 of newborn deaths are preventable. About 5.3 million children are born yearly in Nigeria: that is about 11,000 every day. 1 million of these children will not celebrate their 5th birthday because they are snatched by death.

I found that violence or threat of it, along with accidents on one hand and illnesses on the other hand, constitute what cause residents in Nigeria immediate significant health-related problems and challenges. Of illnesses, rampant infection is of great concern. Food borne infections such as typhoid and poisoning bacteria or their toxins are major threats to lives of the people.

This is not surprising, as I have written earlier, in respect of access to potablewater and good sanitation still being major struggles for the majority of Nigerians. Malaria-causing mosquitoes are ubiquitous. Sanitation is poor as is trust in public potable water. The solution however, is in your hands if you are to avoid being struck down by these agents of death. It is advisable that you only trust the good names of water producers and food sources, or you should firmly decide not to eat beyond your home if, yourself, domestic food handlers and the raw food are free of infection. If you delay in seeking, quality health care, you may be playing with something dangerous in this realm. Life is far too cheap here.

The Economy in Brief: Even though economically, Nigeria oscillates at between being the 24th - 25th largest economy in the world and indeed the largest economy in Africa (sometimes depending on valuation of Naira. South Africa may be the largest or second largest but by general recognition, Nigeria is the largest), with Gross Domestic Product (GDP) of US$550 billion as at 2014 assessment. By 2018, this figure US$550 billion, according to UN Data, had fallen to 404 billion. You should take note that on the average, poor Nigerians (about 60% of the Nigerian population) earn less than $2 per day. Agriculture constitutes about 21% of the GDP (World Bank Data of 2017). For more information, go to
https://data.worldbank.org/country/nigeria
http://data.un.org/en/iso/ng.html)

Government of Nigeria: Nigeria is a federation with 36 States and a Federal Capital. The country runs a presidential type of democracy generally patterned after the United States of America. Having obtained its independence from Britain in October 1960, Nigeria has oscillated between military dictatorship and democratic governance. Since 1999 however, there seems to be some level of stability in the democratic governance in the country. In the early parts of the democratic dispensation, to a keen observer, it was difficult to differentiate between military personnel and the professional politicians because the retired military men simply changed garment to civilian garment and then continued to rule. However, there has been a gradual dilution of the legacy of military presence in the democratic dispensations, in recent times. There is nonetheless one commonality to both military and civilian, which lingers and that is: disregard for the rule of law by both military and democratic governments.

Beyond Fears

The *politics* of Nigeria and the politicians are as diverse as the number of ethnic groups in Nigeria. Various attempts have however been made by law and even by the more pragmatic political arithmetic as well as attempts by the politicians not to be perceived as wearing tags of nativity, tribalism or xenophobic ethnicity. It is very difficult to classify the political doctrines of Nigeria as being to the *left* or to the *right* of political philosophical spectrum such as seen in say in the UK with the Tories or Conservatives on the right and the Labor to the left. Another example is the Republicans in USA to the right and the Democrats to the left of the doctrinal spectrum. Nigeria's political principle is not and cannot even in anyway be identified as being to the Centre. It's nowhere. We are still struggling to get organized and hence identifying a party's philosophy as either left or right does not seem so important right now.

It seems from my personal observation that the underpinning principle and what matters most to the politicians and to a sizeable throng of the people that the politicians lead is simply the old and vibrant doctrine of survival of the fittest. Unsurprisingly, that survival requires that the politicians give their political pursuit whatever it takes including the killing of one another or removal of any opposing force in the way, deception, manipulation of the people or party members and utilization of anything, including human lives, to gain political and hence economic power. The reason for this behavior is clear: the prize of winning a political post in Nigeria is phenomenally big. The smallest political and elected office in Nigeria is counsellorship, which is at the Local Government level. Winning, even at this grass root level is a sure ticket to overcoming poverty and the easy redemption of one's financial fortune. In the least, winning, as Nigerians have come to believe, is a sure bet to self-enrichment perhaps in concert or in synergy with others in cahoots. To gain the chair of a local government in Nigeria in the past and current dispensation is, it appears, almost a certainty to financial enrichment without any judicial question.

In Nigerian politics, the higher the level of political office, the greater the chances of more financial fortunes. It is no secret that the State governors in Nigeria wield enormous financial power. These governors control considerable state wealth, which seemingly they dispense as they fit subject to how much the governor can influence the co-conspirators and sycophants. The worst, most probably, of them all is at the Federal level. Any political student will know that in spite of the much talked about balance of power between the three arms of government; Parliament (National Assembly), Executive and Judiciary, the ultimate power rests in the Parliament. Once a party controls the National Assembly, the party controls the government. That much is true everywhere in the world. The Nigerian political class takes this principle of Parliamentary control, to a different level. This will be further explained under the judiciary and failings of the judicial system. The National Assembly is a law unto itself. Thus, having the constitutional power to override the executive by a two-third majority of votes in a legal enactment opposed by the executive, the National Assembly can make any law that favours its members and especially on financial matters. Therefore, the Nigeria's National Assembly can hold the executive to ransom, make laws to earn unspeakable income that is exponentially disproportionate to the minimum wage in the country and such unreasonable self-protective measures very often go unquestioned in any court of law. This is the reason why the legislators in Nigerian earn about US$40,000 per month while the majority of Nigerians earn $2 per day and national minimum wage is

$60 per month. Below is a commentary by Council on Foreign Relations (www.cfr.org).

In the run up to national elections (scheduled for 2019), there is once again an uproar over the size of the compensation paid to Nigerian parliamentarians. This time, it was Senator Shehu Sani, from Kaduna and a member of President Buhari's All Progressives Congress, who blew the whistle. The Senator divulged the information that the salary of Senators was 750,000 naira per month inclusive of allowances to the tune of 13.5 million naira monthly, making a total package of 14.25 million naira per month. At the current black market rate of 360 naira to the U.S. dollar, that total is slightly less than $40,000 per month, and slightly less than $480,000 per year. (Estimates are that the majority of Nigeria's population live on less than $2.00 per day.)

The Nigerian media has long reported that Nigerian parliamentarians are the most highly paid in the world. Comparison with compensation paid to U.S. senators and representatives might be instructive. U.S. senators or representatives earn a salary of $174,000 per year.

Baring premature death or misfeasance that offends the political class, a legislator at Federal level has financial security for life even if such a legislator chooses to live in any advanced economy of the world, post-legislative era. Being a convicted criminal is not a disqualification to entering Nigerian National Legislative Assembly. The attraction of money and power means transgressions can be covered up at the dictates of political necessity.

The survival instinct rather than a true desire to serve the people among the political class and the lack of credible principles that define party politics is further manifested in the "cross carpeting" that has characterized the politics of Nigeria from inception. Even today, few if any politician at all, can truly be defined by his or her political doctrinal belief. The political terrain is fluid, dynamic, treacherous, uncertain and unprincipled.

On the other side of the spectrum, the reason for the "do or die" political practice in Nigeria is that the power in politics is a liberating force from poverty as mentioned earlier, fear of poverty, desire to dominate others and with the potential for upward trajectory to an upper echelon of society. Seemingly, once power is in one's grasp at whatever level and by whatever means it takes, one must do all that is possible not only to acquire wealth but also to dominate others even in a most brutal way. It has to be said that some of the politicians are already economically successful in their own right before entering into politics.

Furthermore, a cursory look at the political dynamics in Nigeria shows that, as a standard with exceptional few, politics in this realm is a case of winner takes it all. By merely winning, a victor can become fabulously rich or as one Christian preacher in Nigeria, once described himself, a political election upstart winner can become "dangerously" wealthy on a go. Losers lose all. By going into politics, an aspirant stands to lose his life, home, family and wealth or all combined either he or she wins the political post is irrelevant. The game is a high-risk Russian roulette, poker game.

Culture: It's very difficult to define what Nigerian Culture or cultural heritage is at the national level. For example, isn't a nation's unity and coherence defined by the mere ability to assemble a national philharmonic orchestra? Nigeria cannot put together a national symphonic orchestra. The reason for this difficulty stems from and indeed reflects the fact that there are three dominant ethnic groups identifiable by language in Nigeria. As earlier stated, sandwiched between these three are over 250 other ethnic groups with their own languages or dialects and hence their own cultures. All of these groups intermingle to produce some poorly defined cultural identity for Nigeria. One must also mention that each of the thousands of towns and villages in Nigeria have their own religious deities and affiliations notwithstanding the dominance of Christianity and Islam overall. This cocktail of intermingled people makes the definition of the national cultural heritage of Nigeria a herculean task. It seems, the best approach is to identify a Nigerian by his or her own proximal ethnic origin or how the individual wishes to be identified.

Nevertheless, there are some commonalities amongst Nigerians. We all are very religious with a few exceptions who may not even dare to publicly identify themselves as atheists. A Nigerian will either be a Muslim, Christian or belong to a local traditional religion according to the deities of his village or ethnic group. An individual may also hypocritically and surreptitiously belong to all religions and belong to none specifically in reality. The main driving force is where his or her current pressing problems will be solved expeditiously. Wherever that solution may be is the mainstay of religion at least for the time being. We should remember that, whenever there is a run to religion, spread and rise in religious enthusiasm, the trend tends to correlate with a time of personal or collective pain and suffering. Such times may be times of war, times of uncertainties such as examinations or temptations, bereavement or grief, political instability as well as periods of economic hardship, personal and collective vulnerabilities.

Beyond Fears

Just as a typical Briton will talk about the weather, a typical Nigerian will talk about money problems or blame the national leadership for his or her own personal challenges. In similar manner, all Nigerians resident in Nigeria or in Diaspora talk about the poor state of infrastructure especially energy supply that is rationed as well as the poor state of roads and transportation challenges. It seems that expression of gloom and lamentation is a national cultural past time in Nigeria. Sports is a strong rallying point for all Nigerians when all sorts of diverse individuals come together in temporary unity and all differences are temporarily set aside. This is even so, if the national teams especially in football (soccer) are doing well internationally.

That said, I have to admit, Nigerians are a group of lively people. Nigeria is situated on the West Coast of Africa, lies on latitudes 4° north of the Equator and longitudes 3° and 14° on the east of the Greenwich Meridian. It shares boundaries with The Republics of Benin and Niger in the West, Cameroon in the East, Niger and Chad in the North and the Gulf of Guinea in the South, according to NNPC (Nigerian National Petroleum corporation: http://nnpcgroup.com. That means, the country is, in a 24-hour period, served with a minimum of 12 hours of intense sunshine every day of the year, come rain or harmattan. The result is that our skin is charged and changed by the Sun rays, our hormones are super active and our physical body becomes incredibly energised. Thus, we are so easily irritable, angry and loud even when we are not angry, in our approach to one another other. Combined with our lawless state and frustrated by impunity inherent in the system, in addition to the status of "survive or perish" doctrine, it is no wonder that Nigerians are always so impatient.

Beyond Fears

Even if one is in a state of penury, there is usually an expression of hope so much that within the last decade, Nigeria was once given the trophy as the "happiest nation" on earth. The Guardian in 2011, (www.theguardian.com) reported the event thus: *"Nigeria is beset by poverty, corruption and violence – but a poll says it is the world's most optimistic nation"*

This is, in Nigerian parlance and to quote Fela Anikulapo Kuti, a material demonstration of "suffering and smiling" scenario. In spite of the manifold problems in Nigeria and what in other cultures could have been considered as life threatening or even suicidal, majority of Nigerians are hardworking, turning as it were, stony-deaf ears to the shout of corruption and national decadence. One may also safely say, having been grossly frustrated by the national failures, the people have developed thick skin against abuses and frustrations, and have resigned to seeking pleasure wherever they can find it: pretending religiously, that "all is well" and hoping for a better future in spite of never ending national leadership debacles that are distilled to individual's misfortunes. Nigerians as a people are individually focused, pursuing their daily living with vigour with a view to surviving the treacherous economic and frequently apprehensive-generating, ghastly political-economic terrain. They have made reasons to be focused and hard-working.

In this clime, there are no welfare benefits, no social security, unemployment, housing nor healthcare benefits. In addition, there are huge responsibilities staring every Nigerian in the face to the extent of making one prone to developing high blood pressure (a common illness that I see so frequently amongst patients coming to my healthcare facility). Other fears include, housing cost, educational fees for children and the fear of falling ill. Nigerians, being so deeply religious pray daily for the continuing good health of the family bread winner. This is the reason for the high dependency rates that was mentioned earlier. Nigerians in their majority remember every second of the day and in each night, that there is no safety net for them in times of adversity. While this economic condition is perverse, it has given rise to another cultural behaviour: *hustling* or in nice words "struggling" to make ends meet. This is the primary and cultural focus of all and this behaviour of hustling is a critical factor that accounts for almost all of the other good or bad behavioural traits that can be identified with Nigerians.

Strangely, perhaps under the influence of religion and natural instinct to survive, majority of Nigerians behave themselves and keep the law.

Furthermore, notwithstanding a person's financial condition, weddings, funerals for a recently deceased as well as "re-awakening" of the dead or "turning the side" of the long dead is often celebrated in a big party and extravagance at least in sizable regions of the country. You will see a lot of this pomp and pageantry in Lagos and its neighbouring states. Religious affiliation and one's educational level is no barrier. After all, this practice of "turning the dead" is a cultural practice that cuts across a lot of the people of Nigeria but not necessarily all. Thus, a poor person may even borrow to throw a big party or to be seen to have done "the right thing" by being extravagant at weddings and funerals as well as house warming parties and during child naming ceremonies. To this list should now be added school graduation events and conferment of chieftaincy titles on a person: these are excuses to display wealth, show some splendour and pageantry or in the least a moment to forget the frustrations and national failings.

There are bad eggs in every society and country. Nigeria is no different. The bad eggs most frequently are the ones in leadership who may have escaped justice. Yet, there are also some minority individuals that act to criminally tarnish the name of the country. This act of tarnishing may have gone on for too long to become a cultural identity that is projected by the world upon every Nigerian irrespective of if one is a bad person or not. Everyone is thus guilty for the sins of the few.

Thus, lawlessness, lack of justice or injustice and impunity have seemingly become a pervasive cultural issue. This perception is especially so with numerous unresolved political killings and so many people that have lost their lives without justice being served on perpetrators of these hideous crimes.

All of the observations mentioned above do have consequences: words and actions produce results. To all of the bad behaviour and poor image of Nigerians on the global stage, it would be important to add some events that began in the 1970s. Due to the pressure to meet one's daily survival requirements, coupled with Nigerians witnessing impunity by the leadership go scot free, and with the people seeing the rise of easy money from politicians knowing that there is no state social support system; Nigerians have come to realise that the entire Nigerian system supports survival of the fittest. In addition, the Nigerian system favours the strong to the detriment of the weak. Thus, Nigerians are quick to want fast access to money even without meriting such access. All these short-comings have permeated the society. It seems therefore, there is no need for hard, diligent work. Apparently, patience does not pay, and neither does endurance at labour. People get away with criminalities, so why shouldn't I? One may ask. Therefore, a very dangerous, vicious and unfortunate cultural cycle was established and has become the norm in Nigeria today.

Computing and internet technologies which are meant to make our lives much easier have become tools of crime in the hands of fraudsters who practice *Advanced Fee Fraud or 419*. Examples are widespread duping of unsuspecting victims of their money locally and internationally. I have by virtue of some fortune or luck escaped from being a victim of 419ers. 419ers come in various degrees. There are small and big players with god-fathers sitting behind the scene. It's also very difficult to completely escape the grip of fraudsters. Let me cite an example. I saw an air purifier on a Nigerian commercial website. The seller's condition was that I should make a deposit and the item will be delivered to me at home. I followed this instruction on allegedly, a website that appeared credible. The product never came. I called the seller who instructed that we meet up somewhere to collect the item. I sent an assistant to go ahead for the collection. To cut a long story short, the seller who claimed to have a shop in an open mall, never did, and was in fact about 500km away from where he said we should meet up. Once I discovered that I had been defrauded, I immediately wrote a letter to the bank where I made the initial deposit alleging that the bank is a conduit for criminal activity and further that the bank is acting as a conspirator for fraud. The bank took action: they looked at the alleged bank account and immediately suspended it until the owner showed up at a local branch of wherever he may have been or until I, as a victim got paid back. Seeing the magnitude of the money that he was to lose and he not being able to deposit further

419 money into the account, I was paid in full by the 419er within 24 hours of his bank account being suspended. On more inquiry by the bank, he said, it was a third party that used his account to defraud people. He claimed that he "innocently" offered his account to the god-father who remained in the shadow and who also maintained his status of being the power behind the throne. I have lost small amounts to 419 scams, not out of greed but out of ignorance on how to deal with Nigerians. I was green and being a rookie. That was then. Hopefully it will not happen again. I have had several ridiculous offers via the phone or email or letters. I just ignore them now or block the senders. Nevertheless, 419ers will keep testing your boundaries and your security.

Unknown to perpetrators of crimes and the lax law enforcement that ought to curtail these crimes, this negative aspect of the society has serious implications for would-be business investors in Nigeria. The negativity has impact on would be Nigerian residents: creating fear and breach of trust on every front.

When dealing with Nigerians at official or public levels, unless you are familiar with the intrigues of local language and manoeuvring, it is advisable that you get an "elderly" individual or one who is versed in negotiations and in local customs to help you ease or navigate your way around. Overseas/Foreign attitudes and beliefs may not be applicable here and could be considered offensive if they contradict the local customs, norms and beliefs. Nigerians seem to cherish some secrecy, orality (absence of written documentation), personal business approach (as opposed to official contact) as well as some humility (even if the humility or submission is hypocritical) to seniors, elders, authority or to people in power. The same advice is applicable in private or family discussions. In contrast to Europeans or Westerners, looking straight into the eyes of a senior person during a discussion is seen as being disrespectful. You should show your submission (which may be insincere) by slightly bowing your head, and if standing up, in a manner similar to the Japanese way of respect. In the Western world, looking straight into a person's eyes expresses honesty and confidence. Avoiding eye contact in the Western world is interpreted as being illusive and dishonest! You may be seen as disrespectful if you stare into the face or eyes of "elders" here in Nigeria.

There are some behaviour traits that seem peculiar to Nigeria. For example, you sent someone to purchase goods worth say N2000. The messenger may be your ward, family, friend or just an acquaintance. The item is purchased at N1850. Instead of returning the change to you, the messenger may simply keep the change without authorisation. A stranger or visitor to Nigeria may find this bewildering. The solution to the problem is to specifically ask for your change.

Except in supermarkets and very few places, prices on goods and services are not fixed. Nigerian markets are dynamic and sometimes fluid. Sellers expect buyers to haggle and vice versa, towards an equilibrium bargain price. Thus, prices are initially raised to take account of the expected haggle and equilibrium.

Nigerians of whatever religious inclinations will often call for prayer at almost all official and informal meetings. So don't be surprised if prayers are called for at airports, board meetings, and business staff meetings, in market places, political manipulation gatherings, meeting of thugs and civil disobedience strategy meetings. Supplications are also called at political or non-political loot sharing tactical conventions and so on and so forth. Only God knows whose prayers the Maker himself answers: perhaps it's the prayer of the winner or of the one who returned home unharmed. A warning though; be vigilant not to be exploited under the guise of a prayer or being subdued into a state of vulnerability. Maintain your vigilance whatever the case. Subtly exit if you have to. Many people have lost valuables even whilst in church or the mosque with the thieves or enemies in the midst.

In Nigeria, the encounter between doubting Thomas and Jesus illustrates the relationship that should exist between an investor (call the investor, Thomas) and project executor or one who may be receiving money for a project in Nigeria. Owner of work (the client) should standby at site of work to ensure that everything is properly executed as desired, including full, safe, functional, beautiful, durable, and complete quality of work prior to parting with business money. Reassurances of "don't worry" are often false or that 'the work will be done' is frequently a recipe for disaster. This act of cheating is pervasive with both professionals and vocational workers.

Yet another cultural behaviour that may shock anyone is the issue of confidential information. Confiding in a Nigerian is risky business. A limited exception may perhaps be found within certain professionals whose professional conducts are enshrined in law: they include healthcare and legal professionals. Caution: subtle lawlessness is pervasive in Nigeria so even the limited exception that is mentioned should still be handled with caution. While the going is good, the information may be held in confidence. The person who confided in another is at risk of being held hostage or blackmailed when the friendship falls out in the day of adversity. The confidential information may now not be so confidential between friends if power gain or financial benefits or ransom is at stake. Confidential medical information may be leaked to the public, as we saw in Lagos State political intrigues in late 2018. In the case of Lagos State, two aspirants were in a race for the Chief Executive Officer of the State (the Governor). Suddenly, one of the contestants revealed to the shocked public, the confidential medical information of the other. The question is: how did it all get to this? Even where there is no malice, the confidential information may be carelessly disclosed during a *tête-à-tête* with a third party.

In summary, there are three things that are driving the character and culture of Nigeria and also help to form, general outsider's perceptions of Nigeria as a corporate entity. One is lawlessness and laziness with attendant pervasive impunity carried out by the powerful and the less so powerful citizens. The second is the overriding individual's struggle for survival with pursuit of money with a "whatever it takes" attitude to get the money. Third is the knowledge by practically every adult Nigerian that, in so far as Nigeria is concerned, there is no love, "no one cares" for another or that there will be no state support in times of personal need and whatsoever adversity may befall one. "You are on your own" is a daily reality in Nigeria.

Nigeria Legal System.
With very few modifications, the legal system in general falls within the Common Law pattern and jurisdiction as bequeathed to the country by Britain during and after colonisation and independence of the Country. One notable difference is that, in Nigeria there is no such institution as a

County Court that deals with civil matters. Rather, Nigeria has a Customary Court that was set up to deal with disputes arising from issues relating to traditional customs and cultures. An example of such traditional issues would be marriage conducted under the respective custom rather than under Matrimonial Causes Act (Registry/Court Wedding). The dissolution of such traditional marriage will commence at the Customary Court. Registry marriage goes to the High Court.

Nonetheless, while Britain continues to modernise her judiciary system, Nigeria has a lot of archaic laws that are out of "synch" with modern times. One notable example in the British legal system is the use of Practice Directions (PD) that let litigants and defendants in either civil or criminal justice systems know their duties and responsibilities to the Court and to the parties that are involved in the litigation or prosecution process. Evidence to be used in court are disclosed to each other before the court hearing. As a result of the PD, "ambushing" the opponent is not allowed in modern UK legal system. Also, the United Kingdom uses a jury system, albeit with recent unsuccessful attempts in the UK to limit the use of a jury system in some cases. The United Kingdom has legal aid though access to legal aid has now been considerably limited. The United Kingdom has a culture of revision of old laws to keep them up to date. In contrast, element of surprise or presentation of evidence not previously disclosed to the opponent is common in Nigeria. No legal aid or jury system is used in Nigeria. The consequence is that often, in Nigeria, justice is simply not served. This is not to mention the wanton or the common practice of a powerful litigant's total disregard for an unfavourable judgement pronounced by a competent court of law.

As a guide nonetheless, the following describes the structural set up of the legal system in Nigeria.

In general, the structure begins with the Magistrate court at the bottom echelon. Next is the High Court, then comes the Court of Appeal and finally the Supreme Court tops the ladder. Tribunals (usually Special Tribunals) may have the status of High Courts. Customary court fits in between Magistrate courts and High court and it deals with civil matters.

Case Laws: In whatever legal jurisdiction within the country a particular case may fall, once a case gets to the court, the court will make a decision on the case presented to it. The reasoning or lack of it, along with the decision of the court constitutes the *case law*. If the case is new and has never been decided upon, the court decision becomes a *precedent* for other courts of similar status to follow. The higher the court, the higher the order of the lower court to consider and follow precedents of the higher courts.

The Nigeria Judicial Council (NJC) deals with recommendations of judges for appointment to the President of the Country who then makes the final selection and appointment. The NJC also deals with the discipline of Judges.

According to The NJC: *"The National Judicial Council is one of the Federal Executive Bodies created by the 1999 Constitution of the Federal Republic of Nigeria. Amongst other functions, it is responsible for the Appointment, Promotion and Discipline of Judicial Officers. The Council has through various Reforms ensured that it protects and preserves the sanctity of the Judiciary. It is our desire to foster a justice system that is fair, speedy and meets the hope of all men"* (https://njc.gov.ng/).

However, the events of 2018 (and way back before 2018) in Nigeria linking some high ranking judges and justices to corruption (and hence criminal charges) leaves a sour taste in the mouth of Nigerians with the result and perception that there could possibly be no justice or fair play for Nigerians in the legal system. Of course, it is understood that this pernicious suspicion, has been a long held view among the people of the country. There are many reasons to be suspicious.

Notwithstanding, any group of people can, under the Constitution of Nigeria, form an association. The lawyers in Nigeria are no different and thus have an umbrella Association of their own: Nigeria Bar Association (NBA). Except as may be allowed for by the Court Procedures or existing law or by contract, legal cases usually begin at the lowest court as may be appropriate and then go through the court pyramid up to the Supreme Court.

Nigeria is a member of the Economic Community of West African States (ECOWAS) and Community Court of Justice (of ECOWAS). Of particular importance, the Court of Justice has jurisdiction amongst others: to determine cases of violation of human rights that occur in any Member State (including Nigeria). (See: http://www.courtecowas.org). Nigeria is also a member of African Court on Human and Peoples' Rights (See http://www.african-court.org/en/).

I have written all these to lessen the culture-shock that you may experience in Nigeria. This write up, though not exhaustive, is to help you separate facts from fiction.

Chapter 2

Infrastructure: The Nigerian Plague
Failures in Legal, Transport, Healthcare, Housing and Water Systems. Communication, Energy /Power Supply, Education, Security, Commerce including Official Registry, Financial and Credit System.

Before exploring the urgent issue of infrastructure, residents and intending business people in Nigeria must understand some basic facts. Firstly, with some exceptions, we, Nigerians, it seems, hate the law or any order that regulates or restricts our operations or conducts. This is even evident in the various attempts to formally or informally bend or disregard enacted laws. Secondly, except perhaps for a few, we as a people and mostly individually, want to make a gain with minimal effort or no effort at all. By whatever name this latter observation may be called, it is the reason for our strong oral tradition, oral expression and fervent religious enthusiasm with little pragmatism. The first (lawlessness) and the second (of oral expression for gain without effort) points combined, gives rise to deception (advanced fee fraud for example), impunity (such as random, harassment and pre-determined assault of others as well as corruption in public and private places) and the lawlessness that pervades the society and our business ethics. Some specific areas of concern are hereby looked into.

Legal System Failures
It seems reasonable to begin this chapter with the failings of the Nigerian legal system. There is no doubt that the root of all the problems in Nigeria can be traced to the failings in the legal system. Thus, one can say with some degree of confidence that the fundamental problem with Nigeria is

lawlessness. Lawlessness breeds impunity, chaos, violence, corruption, disobedience and arbitrariness. No credible progress and or development can be made in the environment of unruliness. But then, what is lawlessness? Let me offer a simple definition. There are occasions where I argue this issue on my peer forums and I put forward the observation that lawlessness is at the heart of "Nigerian factor" of problems. It seems to me by the response that I get in return, that I have invited controversies. Some responders argue that Nigeria does have laws and the nation is not devoid of laws. These responders fail to understand the subject of lawlessness.

Lawlessness is not to imply lack or absence of laws. Lawlessness means disregard for the laws: which include partial or total disdain for spirit (the purpose of law and the harm to be prevented), the letter and implementation of laws: disobedience to laws and contempt for the supremacy of rule of law.

Any first time visitor to Nigeria will be in awe to see some very strange but very common behaviour with wanton disregard for the laws and common sense: they are what may seem like simple behavioural occurrences such as riding a motorcycle against on-coming traffic, driving vehicles of any sort against on-coming traffic on any road whatsoever, despite the real and intending dangers to offenders. Crossing red traffic lights is another example of some simple lawless behaviour in public. Rules of vehicles stopping at Zebra Crossing for pedestrians does not work. You stand to be knocked down as a pedestrian if you are careless or believing that the vehicles may stop for you. They just zoom away regardless. By extension, notwithstanding an obvious sign on the road, a typical Nigerian driver on the road is likely to flagrantly disrespect the road signs and conduct himself in a manner of impunity. This is just the tip of the iceberg. Driven by survival instinct and operating in an unruly environment, nothing is beyond a Nigerian to convert to his benefit, no matter what the law says.

This is why judges can allegedly take bribes to pervert the course of justice. For the same reason, the government at all levels can allegedly disregard a court order and not carry out a court judgement that is unfavourable to their cause. For the same reason of lawlessness, citizens have taken the law into their hands to murder by mob lynching acts or by any other means, a suspected thief who may have stolen a microfraction of what the powerful have stolen. For the same reason are human beings allegedly redeemed in ransoms and human parts made in sacrifices without repercussion for the offence. For the same reason are offences such as rape and assault committed by clerics acting in the name of God going unpunished. It's for the same logic of impunity that individuals are criminally deprived of their personal and landed property without legal consequences. For the same reason that police that are meant to protect do so allegedly often by brutal abuse, threaten to abuse or kill and extort money from the very citizens that they are meant to protect.

I have had several personal experiences of police abuse of citizens. For example, there was a day I left Lagos at about 6 pm with the aim to get to Ibadan which is just 161 km away from Lagos. I had a seminar to attend where I would deliver a lecture the following day, hence the reason I left a day before. It was a rainy season and the roads as usual, were bad. My work colleague who was going with me in the same car had encountered a little traffic, something not unusual on this road. Just about 40 km before Ibadan at approximately 8 pm a police checkpoint was stationed in the middle of the thick forest, in pitch darkness. The only evidence of human presence were the passing vehicles. We were unfortunate to be stopped. Our offence: I was driving a car, which bore a different number plate from where I was resident. The police officer, who was carrying a gun and heavily drunk and smelling of alcohol, took all my car papers and found nothing wrong. He nonetheless decided that we would only be released on the condition that he sighted a vehicle which bore a similar number plate as my own. Obviously, this was a wild statistical improbability. When I protested, he threatened that he could have me killed. He stated that he would put guns and rifles in my car, so that if he got caught on charge of murder, he would claim that he found the guns in my car and that I was resisting arrest. I will leave the rest of the events to the reader's imagination. Then, the wisdom of the ancient came to me: that indeed, the dead do not have a chance to defend themselves. I had to "settle" the police officer, a daily practice by Nigerians that wish to get home safely.

My own experience, one of many that I have come to be involved in are nothing compared to experiences of some unfortunate persons that have paid dearly for alleged trumped-up police charges.

The Police that Nigerians so frequently complain about and are feared cannot solely be blamed for the illness of Nigeria. They, the law enforcers are just a part of the whole. They also operate in a society that is mired in lawlessness and impunity. The Nigerian police go on international peace keeping assignments and they get awards for good practice. The question is: Why should members of Nigerian police who are singled out ever so now and then for excellent conduct outside Nigeria during international missions, arrive their home nation and become less concerned about law as I have experienced and explained above? Thus, each of the mentioned Nigerian returnee keep the law where they are coming from (overseas) but misbehave even at a Nigerian airport. They diminish in anger and dismiss in frustration anything in sight that is associated with Nigeria. It's for the same reason that lawyers allegedly collude with criminals to escape justice. The same reason of lawlessness that a purported lawyer in charge of trust and testament can convert an estate to his own. The same reason that rape of women and sexual and physical abuse of children go unchecked. Those who are in charge of protecting and defending human rights are at the very core of abusing the trust. This is Nigeria. No love. No care. We are in lawlessness. It has become a culture, our culture and is now ingrained in the national genes: now being passed from one generation to the other. The mantra is survival of the fittest.

Generation upon generation of innocent and perplexed Nigerians observe these events, read about or witness them and then sadly, get some immunity to the lawlessness that surrounds them. No reason to regard the law as sacrosanct seeing that their ancestors thrived on impunity and lawlessness.

Hope is dashed as honest people struggle against the herculean task of unruliness. There is no logic and no benefit to obey the law or as the expression goes, you may obey the law to your peril: "you will stay long in the queue". Being kind and being lawful are perilous undertakings in Nigeria, apparently. If you are kind in Nigeria, friends and family, the public and even those meant to protect your interest see you as weak and ripe for exploitation. It seems that wickedness in a cultural trajectory is beneficial in this land. Criminals and crimes pay, it appears: after all, access to justice is tortuous and there is no guaranty of success if you ever head to court for redress, at the end. So long as you have a connection to a higher "power" of persons in authority, your misbehaviour will be a forgotten issue. Justice delayed, is in essence, justice denied. Cases in courts may last for years and decades before resolutions. Litigants and defendants may have deceased in the process of legal troubles. Therefore, the vicious cycle of lawlessness-injustice-impunity continues with fatal effects on the welfare and well-being of the people as well as the image of Nigeria within and outside the country's frontiers.

Because of threats to individual survival and the absence of justice, our sense of values has been seriously impaired. Nothing is considered precious, save anything that can immediately be turned into money to keep up with the survival instinct. Nothing of enduring value is nurtured for posterity. Therefore, there can only be one outcome to lawlessness and impunity: chaos or state of subdued ignitable violence that seems to cause a majority of Nigerians so much apprehension day and night. Violence can break out at the least excuse. Aggression can be instigated by disgruntled politicians or a wealthy or powerful local or regional thug sheltered by the political class. The law in Nigeria, you remember is meant for the weak, the innocent and the people unconnected to the higher powers "above." In the end, instigators and perpetrators of crimes will get away with their illegality. Evil begets evil. The cycle of lawlessness continues. In Nigeria men and to some extent women rule rather than the law.

Beyond Fears

The Transportation Mirage

At the outset of the book, it was stated that the land mass of Nigeria is just under a million square kilometers in size. Nigeria has a population with high fecundity as mentioned earlier with an estimated population that is approaching 200 million people. One should expect that such a huge human and land resource should have a good transportation system network in place for the people. In addition, one should expect that such a logistic enterprise would keep all levels of government awake and alert, night and day. Unfortunately, at best, the "network" is rudimentary and appears unplanned. The most recent estimate of the total number of motor vehicles in Nigeria as at June 2018 was just about 12 million according to Nigerian Bureau of Statistics (NBS). That is about one vehicle for every 20 Nigerians. Compare that figure to 1:3 in the UK owning a car. Here is the report according to Guardian (Nigeria: https://guardian.ng).

Nigerian Bureau of Statistics (NBS) has estimated the total number of vehicles in the country at about 11.7 million with commercial vehicles holding about 58.08 per cent of the number. According to the report, out of the 11,653,871 million vehicles, commercial vehicles are 6,768,756, representing about 58.08 per cent; private are 4,739,939 (40.67 per cent); government vehicles followed with 139,264 (1.19 per cent); while Diplomatic vehicles accounted for 5,912 (0.05 per cent).

To give us a perception of the state of roads in Nigeria, let us turn to Vanguard in a report dated 7[th]September 2017. Obviously, the facts speak for themselves.

Beyond Fears

"The Director-General, Infrastructure Concession Regulatory Commission, ICRC, Chidi Izuwah, said yesterday that about 135,000 kilometres of road network in the country remained un-tarred. Mr. Izuwah said this in Abuja at the 2017 Otis Anyaeji and Nigerian Society of Engineers Annual lecture.

"Nigeria has about 195,000 km road network out of which a proportion of about 32,000 km are federal roads while 31,000 km are state roads. "Out of this, only about 60,000 km are paved. Of the paved roads, a large proportion is in very poor, unacceptable condition due to insufficient investment and lack of adequate maintenance."

Investors should take note of this part of the above story:

"Private capital and management expertise will help in this area as has happened in Malaysia, India and South Africa," *he said. He said that Nigeria's investment in road and rail remained low and had led to the continued under development of the country, adding to joblessness and poverty."*
(www.vanguardngr.com) .

To follow through the above, the President of Nigeria signed an executive order thus, according to the Punch Newspaper of 26th January 2019.

""President Muhammadu Buhari signed a new Executive Order 007 on Friday, permitting private companies to fund the construction of major road projects in the six geopolitical zones of the country.

"Through this scheme, companies that are willing and able to spend their own funds on constructing roads to their fac-

tories or farms will recover their construction costs by paying reduced taxes over a period of time. We shall ensure complete transparency in these set-offs.

"I call on other local and international investors, as well as the state governments, to embrace this road infrastructure development scheme.

"I personally invite you to submit viable proposals for more road projects, such that, in time, the scope of this initiative will cover all 36 states of the Federation."

Buhari admitted that funding infrastructure had become a burden the government alone could no longer bear, a reason for the new initiative.""

What about rail transportation networks? Compared to Britain, Japan and China, Nigeria has for all practical purposes, no rail network. New initiatives are supposedly being developed to kick-start rail transportation: Nigerian Railway transportation system as at the time of writing this book does not merit writing about.

As for the airports, Nigeria has 30 airports and 26 of these airports are operated by the Federal Airports Authority of Nigeria (FAAN), five of which are functional international airports. It also has a state owned airport located in Akwa Ibom State. In addition, there are airstrips or airfields scattered all around the country, built mainly by the Nigerian Air Force and multinational oil companies. Nigeria has one and the only private public partnership airport operated by Bi-Courtney Aviation Services Ltd. Murtala Muhammed Airport Two (Wikipedia).

However, according to Nigerian Civil Aviation Authority,
"Civil aviation is a critical element in Nigeria's transportation system and indeed its economy. Nigeria has twenty (20) airports and many regulated airstrips and heliports; 23 active domestic airlines; 554 licensed pilots; 913 licensed engineers and 1700 cabin personnel. Nigeria being Africa's most populous country is an important destination for over 22 foreign carriers. Nigeria currently has Bilateral Air Services Agreements with over 78 countries. From Nigeria, air travelers can fly directly to many of the world's business centers such as London, Paris, Frankfurt, New York, Johannesburg, Atlanta, Amsterdam, Dubai and Jeddah to mention a few. With the attainment of America's Federal Aviation Administration (FAA) International Aviation Safety Assessment (IASA) Category One Certification, Nigerian registered carriers can now fly directly into the United States of America (USA)" (http://www.ncaa.gov.ng/).

In general, private participation is very strong in Nigeria's transportation system especially in aviation and road transportation though a lot needs to be done to bring the system to a reasonable standard.

Healthcare in Nigeria
The Healthcare System in Nigeria
This segment will touch on a very important sector that cannot really be avoided by anyone. The Nigeria's Healthcare System can and should be viewed as being pyramidal in structure much like everywhere else in the world. The structure can broadly be divided into primary, secondary and tertiary facilities with the primary, and most commonly found at the base of the pyramid, followed by much fewer secondary facilities and lastly the tertiary that are signifi-

cantly fewer in number than the secondary healthcare systems.

The functional role of primary healthcare is to essentially meet basic health needs and to sustainably serve the local population and offer preventive medicine via health education and vaccination against deadly but preventable diseases. At the primary care level, there are unorthodox or alternative care providers who are both recognized and accepted respectively by the World Health Organization (WHO) and the various governments at all levels in Nigeria

The secondary level, being referral centers for the primary care, is a bit more straightforward as it is where more complex healthcare matters are dealt with. Such centers enjoy the benefit of the presence of multi-specialist medical personnel. They are strategically located in each regional town or local government area as the case may be. In this category are general hospitals, state specialist hospitals, and to some extent, comprehensive medical centers to complete the secondary level of healthcare.

The tertiary facilities are in general teaching hospitals, which are often affiliated to medical schools and colleges. They are frequently part of a larger university with corresponding research facilities. Federal Medical Centers fall between the secondary and tertiary tiers.

The Federal Government's duty or function is mostly limited to coordinating the affairs of the university teaching hospitals and Federal Medical Centers (tertiary healthcare). In turn, the various State governments take care of the various General Hospitals (secondary healthcare) and the Local Government (LG) focus on the primary healthcare centres, which are regulated by the Federal Government via the National Primary Health Care Development Agency (NPHCDA). A lot, if not all of the States have their own Universities and some have affiliated Medical Schools.

Health Insurance

Health Insurance in Nigeria had in the past come under different names at various times or periods. For a while, the government in old Western States of Nigeria guaranteed its citizens free healthcare, which in reality had serious limitations and diluted quality of care.

In May 1999, the Federal Government created the National Health Insurance Scheme, the scheme encompasses government employees, the organized private sector and the informal sector. The scheme also covers children under five, permanently disabled persons and prison inmates. In 2004, the administration of Olusegun Obasanjo further gave more legislative powers to the scheme with positive amendments to the original 1999 legislative act. The number of Nigerians covered by the National Health Insurance Scheme (NHIS) since its establishment is 1.5 percent of the population. So far, the uptake and performance of the Health Insurance is poor. According to publicly available data, barely 10% of Nigerians, mostly middle class have a health insurance. There is immense private sector participation in the National Health Insurance Scheme.

Mental Health

Mental health is a neglected part of the healthcare system in Nigeria. Yet, at least 20% of Nigerians suffer from one mental health problem or another. Most of the problems are denied by sufferers, covered-up by family members, or are ascribed as "spiritual attack" by victims and religious sectors.The majority of mental health service is provided by a few (about eight in number) regional psychiatric centers, psychiatric departments and medical schools of twelve major universities in the country. A few General Hospitals also provide mental health services. The conventional centres often face stiff competition from native herbalists/practitioners and faith healing centers in forms of churches, mosques and traditional healers. I am reliably told that there are some state health regulators that prohibit private medical practitioners from treating mental health victims.

Drug quality is mainly controlled and overseen by the National Agency for Food and Drug Administration and Control (NAFDAC). Several major regulatory failures have produced international scandals. Yet, there are many adulterated and sub-standard pharmaceutical preparations in the Nigerian market. Any drug can be purchased over the counter (without prescription) in Nigeria including antibiotics, narcotics and other controlled substances.

Healthcare in Nigeria is influenced by different local and regional, cultural and religious factors that affect the quality or quantity present in one location. Due to the aforementioned, the healthcare system in Nigeria has shown spatial variation in terms of availability and quality of facilities in relation to needs. However, this is mainly as a result of the level of State and Local Government involvement and investment in health care programmes and education.

Healthcare Personnel
By a conservative estimate, there are about 50,000 doctors on the Medical and Dental Council of Nigeria register list for a population of over 180 million people. The nurses, midwives and allied professionals are correspondingly few

and the population is underserved. The doctor-patient ratio is lowest in the southwest and highest in the Northern part of the country. Retaining health care professionals is an important objective of the government but employment capacity of trained healthcare personnel such as physicians and nurses poses a considerable challenge to the healthcare system.

Migration of healthcare personnel to other countries is affecting the health care system of Nigeria. Many doctors, nurses and allied professionals have emigrated outside the country in search of a better livelihood. The state of healthcare in Nigeria has been exacerbated by a physician dearth because of severe 'brain drain'.

Many Nigerian medical personnel have moved to North America, Asia, South Africa and Europe. As at 2005, 2,392 Nigeria doctors were practicing in the US alone, and in the UK, the number was 1,529. According to *Africa Check* on British Broadcasting Corporation (BBC), the number of Nigerians in the UK's General Medical Council register as at April 2018 has increased to 5,250.

The Role of the Private Sector.
Estimates of private sector participation in healthcare delivery in Nigeria differ overall from one state to another. It might be safe to say that private sector participation in expenditure and in facilities range from 30% to 70% overall. Most of these facilities are located in large industrialized cities, which constitute about 50% of the geographical location of Nigerians. Though informally recognized, many public health workers also work in the private sector.

The Healthcare Laws

As at 2017, there existed some key healthcare sectoral laws enacted as Acts of Parliament or converted from military decrees. The current major healthcare law in Nigeria is the National Health Act, 2014. Also, as mentioned in the *Introduction* there are laws enacted to regulate professionals such as Medical and Dental Doctors. There are similar laws for nurses, pharmacists, physiotherapists and laboratory technicians. Still, there are distinct laws such as *Victims Gun Shot Wounds Act 2017* which impact the healthcare system. Specific laws also regulate the pharmaceutical sub-sector of which the authority of NAFDAC, as mentioned earlier. Specifically, the National Health Insurance Scheme Act, CAP N42 LFN 2004 is the principal law regulating NAFDAC.

Under the National Health Act, 2014, each state may also enact a law to regulate the business of healthcare but it is distinct from regulating the professionals which is done at the federal level. Thus, Lagos State for example has their own Health Reform Law 2006, though predated by the National Health Act 2014, which is nonetheless subject to the Federal Act. The purpose of the State Law is to regulate the business of healthcare delivery and not to regulate the individual professionals.

As can now be seen from the above, healthcare delivery in Nigeria is still largely at a rudimentary and undeveloped stage beset by huge economic, cultural, religious infrastructural and legal issues. Of all the challenges facing healthcare delivery in Nigeria, management of resources and coordination of services between the various players remain a monumental problem. Yet, complaints of negligence by clinicians both in the public and private sectors are rising.
(See: https://www.nipc.gov.ng/overview-healthcare/

Beyond Fears

And
https://oxfordbusinessgroup.com/overview/opportunities-private-companies-nigerias-health-care-sector-and-efforts-improve-provision)

Energy Crisis
In some ways, in Nigeria, corruption in whatever form, may be over-looked by Nigerians in their helpless and maybe hapless ways against the malady of corruption, or be driven into individual and collective sub-consciousness. So can criminal behavior in public places along with some other historical and cultural shortcomings that so frequently bring the country to the fringes of political volcanic eruption.

However, in the entire length and breadth of Nigeria, from the East to the West from North to South, in every land and everywhere there is human habitation in Nigeria, one thing runs across the collective frustrations of the people: energy rationing. It is the most universal, the most proximal, the most painful, the most individual and the economic progress-limiting failing in Nigeria. Energy rationing is the most-talked about problem in the country. A citizen may look the other way in respect of local or national political failings, but who can endure energy inadequacy in an economic pursuit, healthcare service, manufacturing, and engineering and education sector for example, or ordinarily in personal comfort. I must point out to the reader that Nigeria is a hot country no matter where a person lives.

The average temperature is in order of mid-thirties Celsius and a guaranteed 10-12hours of intense sunlight daily. Nigeria is about the 24th largest economy in the world and the largest in Africa. However, Nigeria generates by 2018 data, a meager 7000 Giga Watts (7 Mega Watts) of energy per day. Nigeria has the plains of the Sahel and the Savannah landscapes. It seems Nigeria forgot the power of the wind in the Sahel. The massive coastal areas of the country could generate great amounts of energy for the economy. By various approximations, Nigeria requires a barest minimum of 40 Mega Watts per day. I hope would-be investors have taken note.

In fact, by another projection, for say *"13% GDP growth rate (a very over optimistic figure) the demand projections rose from 5,746MW in the base year of 2005 to 297,900MW in the year 2030 which translates to the construction of 11,686 MW every year to meet the demand. The corresponding cumulative investment (investment & operations) cost for the 25-year period is US$ 484.62 billion, which means investing US$ 80.77 billion every five years within the period*" (According to Matching Electricity Supply with Demand in Nigeria. By A. S. Sambo).

Here is a statement from The Guardian of 8th January 2016:
"Chief Executive Officer, Association of Nigeria Electricity Distributors, Azu Obiayo (left); Managing Director, Benin Electricity Distribution Plc, Mrs. Olufunke Osibodu; and Executive Director, Commercial, Abu Ejoor, at a press conference in Lagos.
The nation's aggregate electricity need has been estimated at about 160,000 Mega Watts (MW) to satisfy the local electricity demand, even as indications emerged that the Electricity Distribution Companies (Discos) may not be able to meet the one year deadline set by the Federal Government to meter all consumers in the country."

If Nigeria is to aspire to become a major world economic power in the top 10, this barest energy requirement needs multiplication in high numbers. Thus, Nigeria is an underperforming nation, not just economically but equally in human capital development, law enforcement and massive energy requirements. To a business minded-individual, this energy lacuna presents a significant business opportunity.

Potable water as a luxury in Nigeria
Notwithstanding the enormous energy needs above, nothing compares to the poor state of water supply in Nigeria. Water supply and energy need go hand-in-hand. I also mentioned in Chapter One, the fact that only approximately 29% of Nigerians have access to good water. Where there is poor energy supply, it is logical that there will be poor water sources to meet the needs of the people. Put in brief, official water supply is limited to few members of the general population in the cities and towns. In rural areas, rainwater, well water, streams and rivers (often-infected rivers) account for a majority of water needs of the people.

The importance of clean and accessible water to the well-being or health of individuals and the general economy of the country cannot be over emphasized.

Granted that few people have access to pipe borne water, it would be very risky to drink the water from such sources. Such water is often not potable as the people are made to believe. Should you decide to take the risk, you stand the chance of contracting deadly infectious diseases such as typhoid and other non-typhoid gastroenteritis. To counter the unreliability of public water supply, many well-known name multinationals have entered the business of "bottled" (actually, plastic) water supply accompanied by innumerable small and medium business enterprises. The names of water suppliers across the country is possibly as varied and manifold as the religious places of worship in the country. If the vigor by which the race to meet drinkable water shortage is applied to energy gaps, the power supply in Nigeria would have largely improved. Yet, the nation still has perhaps, one of the largest typhoid cases, water, food-infected and communicable diseases in the world. To put this problem in perspective using the words of United Nations Children's Fund (UNICEF)

"Poor access to improved water and sanitation in Nigeria remains a major contributing factor to high morbidity and mortality rates among children under five. The use of contaminated drinking water and poor sanitary conditions result in increased vulnerability to water-borne diseases, including diarrhea which leads to deaths of more than 70,000 children under five annually.

Seventy-three per cent of the diarrhoeal and enteric disease burden is associated with poor access to adequate water, sanitation and hygiene (WASH), and is disproportionately borne by poorer children. Frequent episodes of WASH related ill-health in children, contribute to absenteeism in school, and malnutrition. Only 26.5 per cent of the population use improved drinking water sources and sanitation facilities. Also, 23.5 per cent of the population defecate in the open." (www.unicef.org).

I have personally been a victim of typhoid and non-typhoid diseases countless times. I am grateful for being a medical doctor with high index of suspicion which has enabled me to avoid serious damage to my health. Having learnt the lesson of lethal infections with family members, friends and work colleagues dying prematurely of preventable illnesses and being let down by private and public health facilities, individuals have also entered both the water and energy supply business to meet mostly personal, domestic and own business needs. The strategy and its execution are simple. If you can afford a "bore-hole" (which is a more scientific and modern way of reaching the earth's aquifer), get one! The technology is simple and the physical requirement is not much. Being aware of their own failings, the legal requirement from the government is almost nil as at the time of writing. That is, the government puts limited barriers on personal and commercial water enterprises on setting up. On an individual level, setting up a borehole, may set you back by between local equivalent of US$500-3000 depending on where you are in the country and your bargaining power. However, you need a good generator to power the 1-2 horsepower pump that brings the water to the storage tank on the earth's surface. The bore-hole must be deep enough, serviced regularly, and be cited far away from septic tanks (cesspit) or any other contaminant. The big players of water merchants also rely on boreholes that are sunk at uncountable places in Nigeria. Any claim of water in bottle/plastic being from a "natural spring" should be held with a pinch of salt. Depending on your affordability and health inclination as well as location, the borehole water may require "treatment' or purification process before consumption. For certainty, if you have a borehole in Lagos Island or Lekki areas of Lagos State, you may need desalination of the borehole water. Except for hyper-salination and excess iron, most borehole water is suitable for immediate consumption without further intervention. Thus, most of the unopened bottled water is good for consumption but should you wish to go the extra mile, you can purchase the labels of known international beverage and soft drink manufacturers water brands such as Eva by Nigerian Bottling Company (local franchise holder of *Coca Cola*)

Communication
Before 1999, Nigeria had no cellular or mobile phones except for the few very rich individuals who had the luxury of satellite communication, using gigantic handsets of that time. In fact, prior to the advent of widespread use of mobile phones, the available landline then, which was scarce, ineffective and costly to use and obtain, for the Nigerian population of about 90 million, was about 500,000 in number. Thus, majority of Nigerians were "ex-communicated" from each other but were also effectively disfranchised. Business transactions were, as one could imagine slow at best. Banks were clogged with throngs of people. Bank transactions moved at snail speed and one could spend the entire day even into the following day, chasing a counter cheque that required immediate cashing. With the advent of mobile phones in 2001, the communication potential of Nigerians blossomed. As at the time of writing this book, February 2019, and according to Nigerian Telecommunication Commission, NCC, (www.ncc.gov.ng) there were over 98.3 Million internet access subscribers in Nigeria, which translates to about 50% of the population. 248,115,152 lines are connected (GSM, CDMA, VoIP and Fixed or Wireless). Active lines number stood at 169,104,830 according to NCC.

In 2018, the average broadband internet speed in Nigeria was approximately 1.5MB/s making it one of the slowest in the world according to BBC (British Broadcasting Corporation). There are about four major mobile phone service providers in Nigeria (Glo, Airtel, 9-Mobile, MTN) with some smaller ones sandwiched between the four. Cable transmission of internet protocol is yet unknown or available. Therefore, practically all communication goes through the mobile service providers' satellite-based network though the likes of Vodacom uses microwave technology and is available in Nigeria. Similar to the gradual demise of cable telegraphy in Europe in 2019, few organizations and individuals retain their cable-based telephone landlines. Fax machines are for all practical purposes, not in existence in Nigeria as at the time of writing this book. Presently, advanced economies of the Western Hemisphere are phasing out fax machines. Therefore, Nigeria is ahead of the game in some ways.

Thus, like other countries in the world, majority, if not all, means of communication are through mobile phones (voice and instant messages), internet (social media, websites, email and chat apps). Printers still offer scanning capabilities into email and so forth. As to the phone handset market, there is no control and no apparent restriction on entry. Most handset makers are represented in Nigeria (iPhone, Samsung, HTC, Infinix, LG and many others). Barrier to entry seems low though the market itself is a good regulator having brutally shaken some good names (Motorola, Alcatel) out of the Nigerian phone market.

The downside to all of these is the fact that while there are more open communication channels and opportunities in the sector, there is often the problem of downtime as the consumers have come to accept. This acceptance seems to have become a cultural acceptance of phone service providers failure in what service users' call, dismissively as "no service" or giving excuse in defense of the service providers: "its network" problem from the providers. We do not seem to perceive the failures that I have mentioned as gross inadequacies of the service owners who make a phenomenal amount of money from their subscribers. If the "no service", experience, which so frequently occurs in Nigeria had happened or been precipitated by any of the phone service providers in the UK for example, such an occurrence would have resulted in severe official reprimand of the providers and even to the level of financial penalties. In Nigeria however, such an abysmal failure of the phone service providers are not only helplessly accepted by the users as "one of those failings in Nigeria", but also, there is often no report by users to regulators. Even where reports get to the regulators, the consequences for the poor service are not known to the public thus raising the spectre that official regulators do nothing or are in the least allegedly in conspiracy with the mobile phone service providers. Example: (I do have several phones and sim cards all at once. This is cultural here to have multiple service providers). My service provider for an unknown reason, blocked my phone line for about 3 months. After several complaints to the service provider, nothing came forth. So, I wrote to the NCC that regulates the mobile phone companies. Even after several months of lodging my complaint with NCC, no response was ever provided by the regulator. Nigerians have come to accept that in time of crisis (abuse, assault, immigration issues, housing and other challenges), there will be no help to assist them from official quarters. You are on your own. In the end, I had to pursue the restoration of my phone line with the service provider.

Therefore, communication can be abruptly interrupted and transmission of data sharply curtailed with impunity. All said, and to be fair, Nigeria has made some progress in the communications sector though quite a small step compared to the rest of the world's major economies.

Education Systems in Nigeria:

Beyond Fears

Though the educational system in Nigeria suffered a major blow in the past, the current challenges are threefold: Firstly, poor quality, which seems to be because of the ubiquitous and invasive lawlessness in the country. The second problem is inadequacy of educational resources to meet demands against a rapidly growing population, and the third is the historic and concurrent destructive disruptions in public higher institutions. The educational system seems to be under intense pressure from all of these factors.

The educational system was liberalized in modern times and from kindergarten to University, private individuals and organized institutions such as religious bodies could establish and own any educational institution. All are of course subject to respective government approvals and supervisions.

While the private institutions are generally pricier, they provide stability against the disruptions of public institutions. Strikes by workers and industrial disputes can prolong a 3-year University degree course to say 5 or more years before graduation. (At my first degree, I once had an industrial dispute that added five months to my course duration! My lot is still much better than modern students).

Educational resources include Federal Ministry of Education, respective State Ministry of Education, Nigerian University Commission (NUC), Nigerian Educational Research and Development Council (NERDC). All of these bodies have their respective websites though as mentioned elsewhere in this book, *physical presence* of persons rather than internet or telephone and letter communication is still the mainstay of doing business in Nigeria. Apart from physical presence, other means of communication may not elicit a response.

The Financial System.
Nigeria has in general, improved since the mid 2000s world financial crisis, and improved albeit with much more room for greater and better quality financial systems. Public access to complaints and credible response from regulators is lacking. The regulator (Central Bank) needs to do more and to wake up to its responsibilities. I once complained about my bank that withheld my money without a reason. So far no response from Central Bank or to even acknowledge my email or complaint. Again, like millions of Nigerians, I have to shoulder my burden. Never expect help from official quarters.

There are however about 21 commercial banks offering commercial retail services according to the early 2019 data made available by the Central Bank of Nigeria (www.cbn.gov.ng). There are also Micro-finance banks that lend to support petty traders and small businesses. They are so-called Microfinance because these lenders lend very minute amounts to support small businesses, which in real terms were rejected by the mainstream commercial banks. I once used a Microfinance loan to support my business having been rejected by the big commercial banks even when I proposed to accept the unreasonable and unfriendly interest rates offered. My advice would be that one should avoid a loan in Nigerian Financial system whatever it takes. I have seen that the end does not often justify the means here. The debtor may suffer more health issues simply because of the loan and the ridiculous interest rates.

Just as in Europe and USA, there are also, "shark" financial houses lending to businesses and the general public at extremely unreasonable interest rates and strangulating terms and conditions. An impossible situation for start-up busi-

nesses. On the average, the commercial and microfinance banks' lending rate is in the order of 30-35% and above. If this rate is well-regulated, financial institutions can shun out for their clients. It only can be imagined what the annual percentage rate (APR) is for the shark financial houses. I was once offered a 60% interest rate over a loan that was meant to be impossibly redeemed at the third month post lending. Notwithstanding, there are other financial institutions such as Development Financial Institutions (Development Bank of Nigeria (DBN), Bank of Agriculture, Bank of Industry, Nigerian Export-Import Bank and Infrastructure Bank, Federal Mortgage Bank of Nigeria and NERFUND (National Economic Reconstruction Fund). Federal institutions set out to be more generous towards individuals and businesses. The reality is not so, as I found out myself. A proposed DBN loan interest rate that I was once offered ranges between 22-35% by the retail agents that the DBN outsourced their loan service. Besides, some politics may be involved before federal institutions could grant a loan. Full details of the banks are here:
https://www.cbn.gov.ng/Supervision/AllFinInstitutions.asp

Insurance: The state of the insurance industry in Nigeria seems to have improved with the advent of *National Insurance Commission Act of 1997 and the Insurance Act of 2003*. Nonetheless, the uptake of insurance against losses still lags in Nigeria. As at October 2017, there were 28 Insurance Companies in Nigeria providing general insurance. There were 14 insurance companies providing life insurances. Those providing professional liabilities insurances are probably fewer in number. These should not be confused with the Health Management Organization (HMO or "insurance") though the likes of AXA-Mansard crisscross the health and life insurance platforms. For more on the regulation of Insurance Industry in Nigeria, readers should contact National Insurance Commission (www.naicom.gov.ng). On the other hand, HMOs are regulated by the National Health Insurance Scheme (NHIS) that license the HMOs. In the minds of the public, many doubts remain about the sincerity of the insurance industry in supporting premium payers during adverse conditions. For personal injury issues to be adequately addressed in Nigeria the law regulators of the insurance sector should be updated, and the systems of administration be made dynamic in order to meet the aspirations of consumers and reassure the public in a timely fashion. The insurance claim process needs to be speedy, transparent and fair if the public is not to be discouraged on the uptake of insurance protection. Some good news though. Allianz Insurance has by February 2019, entered the Nigerian Market.

Credit Score: Anyone looking for his or her credit score to aid his or her lending from the banks should forget it. Such credit scoring system does not exist for the Nigerian public. That said, the vacuum of credit scoring service is an opportunity for a would-be business entity to start one in Nigeria. I am reliably informed that banks have some cryptic debt recording systems that help them to check on potential loan takers. Of course, there are international credit scoring agents such as Fitch that keep an eye on Nigerian Banks and their liquidity base. Thus, from the perspective of a new business, start-up, Diaspora returnee or even the Nigerian public in general, the saying goes that the Banks are not helpful, and that instead, loans are only given to big boys/girls (big and well connected players) and big businesses. Therefore, just as in the political dispensation, the credit system in Nigeria is a no starter for a minnow. The game is for only the dominant, the powerful, the "politically exposed" and the economic giants: notwithstanding the source of money of the said giants or his ability to pay back the loan. Anyone, especially lesser mortals, either personally or in business who may be seeking a credit facility to finance his or her business or to aid such a person's living in Nigeria is setting himself or herself up for a terrible and painful disappointment. In sum, the Nigerian financial system depends on what citizens have long been accustomed: it is a "cash and carry" system. You have your money; you get the goods or service. No more, no less.

That said, the debit card system is vibrant and dynamic. Anyone can get this facility. In fact, in comparison to developed country, Nigeria scores a first in the issuance of bankcards. The issuance of debit cards by the banks is impressive to say the least. This is so because of the peculiar environment that Nigerians find themselves in and have created and adapted to survive in. Applicants can obtain a debit card on the spot in some banks. The reason for this experience is logical and structural. The authentic personal addressing scheme is not reliable and the official postal system in Nigeria is poor. Lawlessness is rife and financial fraud is high. Delivery of debit cards by established courier will add additional cost of doing business. To be safe, the banks have taken a strategic approach by providing their clients with a value-added advantage in the issuance of on the spot debit cards, upon application.

Another incredible fraud-busting approach is the system of sending "alerts" to bank clients when a transaction takes place on specific bank accounts. While, the bank provides this service on request via a form duly filled by the client, it is advisable that every bank client in Nigeria or in Diaspora access this service of alerts. Messages about each bank transaction are sent to the client's email inbox and an instant message (SMS) is sent to the client's telephone number that is provided by the respective bank. Delivery of alerts depends on good service by the mobile telephone providers. Where there is "no service" there will be no alert. Again, Nigerian banks score a first in this respect of alerting clients of transactions on their accounts.

Security
One of the events that causes most fear is security. As either a newcomer or existing resident, security is a top concern for everyone in Nigeria. In official terms, Nigerian security apparatus consists of the Military, which is made up of the Army, Airforce and the Navy. Some other services including the Secret Service may be an extension of the military. The DSS (Department of State Services) or SSS (State Security Services), NIS (Nigerian Immigration Service) are security agencies of the Federal Government of Nigeria. The most visible of the security set up is the Police Force and lately the Civil Defence Corps. There are emergency response agencies such as Fire Brigades and disaster responders (National Emergency Management Agency, NEMA). Some states have units that control the traffic system and responders to urgent events even though there is the Federal Road Safety Corps (FRSC) and also Vehicle Inspection Officers (VIO). The most visible of security apparatus are the police officers: men and women. A driver is also likely to come across the FRSC and VIO as well as the State-organized traffic officers. The Nigerian Police Force has its own dedicated Traffic Officers who wear a distinct orange top on black trousers. There are also the Immigration and Customs Forces.

Beyond Fears

The security system is not separate from the "Nigeria PLC". They are part of the problems and solutions as is every resident in Nigeria.

The Nigerian police operates within the culture of Nigeria and to know the value of the police, just imagine them being on a strike for a day or two. Without the police force, the whole country will be under the siege of hoodlums, cultists, armed robbers, intimidators, blackmailers, rapists, kidnappers, petty thieves, area boys and girls, ignitable political fuse, and general chaos. The security forces and the police are doing a great job keeping the country safe. However, they are still under the influence of the "Nigerian factor" of overarching behavior, impunity and in some ways a tinge of abuse of power and position. It is surprising though that members of the Nigerian Police Force could win good performance awards during duties outside Nigeria yet face so much derision within its own borders.

Visitors and individuals relocating to Nigeria should not expect similar relationships with the Police as in say in the UK or other countries. Allegedly, under the cloak of abuse, misuse of power, impunity, a simple confidence in some members of the police could result in fatal outcomes especially when monetary values are at stake or if the member of public that is seeking help is in dire or vulnerable position or not well "connected" to protective higher powers. This could happen during the day or night or if the member of public speaks in different foreign accents. Apparently, some elements within the force could misuse confidential information or take advantage of information for selfish gains. Individual police officers could also be used, albeit illegally, to harass neighbors or intimidate a party to a dispute even if the dispute is civil in nature or the dispute does not ever warrant the use of law officers. This latter event is clearly a "show of power" and a demonstration of one's connection to the people in high places of power. I write from personal experience. Similarly, it is risky to argue or overtly disobey or abuse a police officer that carries a gun: after all, a dead victim of gunshot is not in position to argue his case. Even if one is not dead, a simple and arbitrary criminal allegation by a malicious police officer against an innocent and vulnerable person could not only lead to time wasting but also possible incarceration without justice, for the victim. Thus, in general, whilst the police are performing wonderfully within the context and the environment of their operation in Nigeria, one should always remember that the ubiquitous "Nigerian factor" has no limit in its scope of operation.

In the last decade or so, Nigeria has suffered a major religious violent uprising in the Northeast and it is still on going as at the time of writing though much of the chaos has allegedly been contained, apparently. At any given time, Nigeria is never far away from one ethnic pandemonium, religious stampede, national public service labor strikes, one political upheaval or the other. Very often, such disturbance is limited to a small space or the chaos is regional in nature and rarely national with exception of labor strikes that may actually cripple the national economy for a few days or weeks.
One thing seems clear in all these years of the country's existence: the nation and the people are resilient in spite of all the centrifugal forces that seem to tear at it.

Commerce including Official Registries
Nigeria is unique among the nations of the world. There is never a dull moment. The over 250 languages, dialects and numerous religions make Nigeria particularly peculiar and

dynamic. Unofficial markets are always open irrespective of the religious public holidays being currently observed. The reason is simple. When Muslims are celebrating a festival, Christians might sense an opportunity by opening their shops and vice versa for Christian holiday festivals. That is not to erroneously conclude: existence of any interfaith dehiscence. After all, most families and friends have members that belong to different faiths. Therefore, the market is open every day one way or the other. In Lagos, the commercial capital of Nigeria, everyday is business: day and night though commerce may be less intense during major national religious holidays. Given the chance, every space in Lagos may be turned into a commercial activity of some sort. This commercial spirit in Lagos is somewhat replicated in other parts of the country, to a lesser extent.

At the Federal level, there are numerous official regulators and registrars of registered businesses. Some regulations are also subject to the industrial sector where the business operates.

States derive their power subject to Federal power and as may be instituted by the constitution of the nation or the respective enabling laws. Therefore, States may also regulate certain businesses in addition to Federal activities. Of importance is Corporate Affairs Commission (CAC) (equivalent of Companies House in the UK) that registers incorporated businesses and incorporated charities. The full list of Federal regulators and a few for Lagos State are listed the end of this book in the appendix.

The Federal government has tried to simplify or improve the environment for doing business in Nigeria. It has done this by reducing the fee for business registration, allowing online applications and simplifying requirements.

A few words need to be said about official bodies and communication with them. Nigeria still relies on manual ways of doing things and physical presence of individuals who intend to conduct businesses with official bodies. Thus, sending letters by post or even by courier may not elicit a response. An email message may be ignored even if it is delivered and read. Officially, responding to personal or business inquiries is not a norm in this clime as at the time of writing. Private businesses may also not bother to respond to inquiries or business requests with exception of a condition: if there is a monetary gain from such an inquiry, then response may be swift. For both government and non-governmental services/product providers, customer concerns may not provoke a reply.

Indeed, government offices or agencies expect inquirers and persons seeking information or seeking to transact business to show up physically. It appears as if the seeker of information is receiving a favour. The reason for this awkward situation is clear at closer inspection. The more information that is hoarded the greater the sale value to the likely seller. Similarly, with a history of strong oral expression and long history of official secrecy, the less that is committed to paper, the more the lack of evidence to back up a potential claim by claimants. Thirdly, power is intoxicating. The question might go thus: *"Why can't I in my position of power or (ir)responsibility, sit back in my office so that information seekers and members of the public, low and high business people come to my office to pay me obeisance rather than engaging in writing or responding to inquiries via email or conventional letter?"* Is that an evidence of laziness or power domination or abuse, lawlessness or sheer irresponsibility? You must have guessed the answer.

Chapter 3.
Nigeria's Business Climate

The Peculiarity of Nigeria. The Incredible and Untapped Opportunities: Potential Power House. Factors Limiting Growth. Regulatory Framework and Business Forms.

"Some people dream of success, while other people get up every morning and make it happen."
---Wayne Huizenga.

To begin with, it is important to put the "ease of doing business" in Nigeria in international perspective. Thereafter, a comprehensive look will be taken at why the Nigerian environment is so hostile to residents and businesses alike. In 2016, Nigeria ranked 169 out of 189 countries in the World Bank Ease of Doing Business Index. One might be tempted to assume that this was a small improvement on Nigeria's ranking. After all, in 2014 and 2015 Nigeria ranked 175 and 170 respectively. Nigeria reached an all-time high of 108 in 2008.

However, by the assessment of World Bank labelled: "DB 2019 Ease of Doing Business Score", Nigeria had dropped to the rank of 146 from the level of 108 in year 2008. As the reader can see, these are many oscillations in the ranking for Nigeria: all of them in the lower half of the ranking table. (http://www.doingbusiness.org/en/data/exploreeconomies/nigeria). In the same ranking for 2019, Kenya was 61 and South Africa was 82. United Kingdom was ranked 9, while Singapore was number 1.

The Peculiarities of Nigeria
Incredible potential. Taking into consideration the numerous topics exposed in the preceding chapters, such topics and

observations create incredible business potentials for would-be businesspersons with the provision of understanding, bearing and enduring what might appear to be insurmountable challenges in Nigeria. One peculiar problem in Nigeria and possibly responsible to some degree of poverty, is lack of cooperation amongst Nigerians to solve a perceived human or environmental problem. Individuals wish to dominate, sit on what they have acquired and to ultimately control others. This perceived selfish reason is also possibly responsible for lack of research, low business uptake, exploration and processing of the earth and environmental resources.

In the early 2000s, I appeared on a television show where I was asked if Nigeria had any potential. I told my host and the listeners that Nigeria is laden with gold, wherever you go. Following the consternation of my host as to my "gold-laden answer", he asked me where the gold was and requested that I show the public where to find it. Well, the gold in my reasoning had nothing to do with the material in chemistry's Periodic Table that has the formula Au. I was referring to the monumental opportunities available to would-be takers and entrepreneurs in Nigeria, which the residents and Nigerians in Diaspora are either hamstrung from taking advantage of or unable to perceive such prospects.

Nigeria, we should bear in mind, is a rose with a manifold of very sharp thorns attached to the beautiful flower. Whomsoever will take the nicely scented and colourful rose, should prepare him or herself to be pierced by the attached barbs. Otherwise, as we all know and Nigeria is no exception, you cannot eat your cake and have it.

In this chapter, the Nigerian business climate and the monumental opportunities that are available within it will be highlighted.

Nigerian Business Climate: The Law
The Federal Government of Nigeria clearly recognizes the enormous difficulties inherent in doing business in Nigeria. To ease the perceived comprehension, a recent Executive Directive promulgation by the Federal Government is hereby reproduced, verbatim.

EXECUTIVE ORDER NO. 001 OF 2017
BY THE ACTING PRESIDENT OF THE FEDERAL REPUBLIC OF NIGERIA

On the Promotion of Transparency and Efficiency in the BusinessEnvironment

WHEREAS, it is the policy of the Federal Government of Nigeria (FGN) tocreate an enabling environment for businesses and entrench measures andstrategies aimed at promoting transparency and efficiency;

WHEREAS, the FGN is committed to the promotion of domestic and foreigninvestments, creation of employment and stimulation of the nationaleconomy; and

WHEREAS, His Excellency, Muhammadu Buhari, GCFR, the President, Commander-in-Chief of the Armed Forces, Federal Republic of Nigeriaconstituted the Presidential Enabling Business Environment Council tocoordinate the implementation of this policy;

NOW THEREFORE, PURSUANT TO THE AUTHORITY VESTED IN ME BY THE CONSTITUTION AS THE ACTING PRESIDENT OF

THE FEDERAL REPUBLIC OF NIGERIA, I HEREBY ORDER AS FOLLOWS:

Transparency in MDAs
1. Every Ministry, Department and Agency (MDA) of the FGN shallpublish a complete list of all requirements or conditions for obtainingproducts and services within the MDA's scope of responsibility,including permits, licenses, waivers, tax related processes, filings and approvals. The list shall

a. include all fees and timelines required for the processing ofapplications for the products and services; and

b. be conspicuously pasted on the premises of the relevant MDAand published on its website within 21 days from the date ofissuance of this Order.

2. It shall be the responsibility of the head of the relevant MDA to ensurethat the list is verified and kept up-to-date at all times. If there is anyconflict between a published and an unpublished list of requirements,the published list shall prevail.

Default Approvals
3. Where the relevant agency or official fails to communicate approval orrejection of an application within the time stipulated in the publishedlist, all applications for business registrations, certification, waivers, licenses or permits not concluded within the stipulated timeline shallbe deemed approved and granted.

4. The mode of communication of official decisions to applicants shall bestated in the published requirements.

5. Where applications are rejected within the stipulated timeline, allrejections shall be given with reasons. Rejections of applications shall be tracked and accurate records kept at all times for each MDA andshall be submitted to the head of the MDA on a weekly basis.

6. There shall be at least two (2) modes of communication of acceptanceor rejection of applications to the applicants by the relevant MDAsbefore the expiration of the stipulated time, including letters, emailsand publications on MDA websites.

7. The applicant's acknowledgement copy of the application, includingelectronic submission acknowledgements, shall serve as proof of thedate of submission of the application for purposes of determination ofthe commencement of the application timeline.

8. An Applicant whose application is deemed granted under thisDirective may apply to the Minister for the time being in charge of theapplication for the issuance of any document or certificate in evidenceof the grant within 14 days of lapse of the MDA's stipulated timelinefor the application.

9. Failure of the appropriate officer to act on any application within thetimeline stipulated, without lawful excuse, shall amount to misconductand be subject to appropriate disciplinary proceedings in accordancewith the law and regulations applicable to the civil or public service.

One Government Directive

10. An MDA that requires input documentation, requirements orconditions from another MDA in order to deliver products andservices on applications within the originating MDA's remit ormandate, including permits, licenses, waivers, tax documentation,filings and approvals shall only request a photocopy or other *primafacie* proof from the applicant. It shall be the responsibility of theoriginating MDA to seek verification or certification directly from theissuing MDA.

11. Service Level Agreements shall be binding on MDAs and shall be reliedupon by MDAs in the issuance of pub-

lished stipulated timelines forprocessing of applications for the products and services.

12. It shall be the responsibility of the head of the relevant MDA to ensurethat the agreed terms of the Service Level Agreements are adhered to.

13. Failure of the appropriate officer to act within the timeline stipulatedin the Service Level Agreement, without lawful excuse, shall amount tomisconduct and be subject to appropriate disciplinary proceedings inaccordance with the law and regulations applicable to the civil orpublic service.

Entry Experience of Visitors and Travellers

14. Ordinary tourist and business entry visas to Nigeria shall henceforthbe issued or rejected with reason by the Consular Office of NigerianEmbassies and High Commissions within 48 hours of receipt of validapplication. The timeline shall be notified to the public by pasting anotice conspicuously at every Consular Office and by publication onevery website of Nigerian Embassies and High Commissions.

15. A comprehensive and up to date list of requirements, conditions andprocedures for obtaining visa on arrival, including estimatedtimeframe, shall be published on all immigration-related websites inNigeria and abroad, including Embassies and High Commissions, andall ports of entry into Nigeria.

16. The processing of issuance of visas on arrival shall be carried out in atransparent manner. Visas on arrival shall be granted at all Nigerianports of entry once applicants have met all the publishedrequirements.

Port Operations

17. There shall be no touting whatsoever by official or unofficial personsat any port in Nigeria. On duty staff shall be properly identified byuniform and official cards. Off duty

staff shall stay away from the portsexcept with the express approval of the agency head. The FAAN
Aviation Security (AVSEC) and Nigeria Ports Authority (NPA) Securityshall enforce this order.

18. All non-official staff shall be removed from the secured areas ofairports. No official of FAAN, Immigration, security agency or Ministry of Foreign Affairs (MFA) or any other agency is to meet any non-designateddignitary at any secure areas of the airport. The officialapproved list of dignitaries that have been preapproved to be receivedby protocol officers shall be made available to AVSEC and otherrelevant agencies ahead of their arrival at the airport.

19. Any official caught soliciting or receiving bribes from passengers orother port users shall be subject to immediate removal from post anddisciplinary as well as criminal proceedings in line with extant lawsand regulations.

20. All relevant MDAs at the airports shall within 30 days of the issuanceof this Order merge their respective departure and arrival interfacesinto a single customer interface, without prejudice to necessarybackend procedures.

21. All agencies currently physically present in Nigerian Ports shall within60 days harmonise their operations into one single interface stationdomiciled in one location in the port and implemented by a single jointtask force at all times, without prejudice to necessary backendprocedures.

22. The new single interface station at each Port shall capture, track andrecord information on all goods arriving and departing from Nigeriaand remit captured information to the head of the MDA and the headof the National Bureau of Statistics on a weekly basis.

23. Each Port in Nigeria shall assign an existing export terminal to bededicated to the exportation of agriculture produce within 30 days ofthe issuance of this Order.

24. The Apapa Port shall resume 24-hour operations within 30 days of theissuance of this Order.

Registration of Businesses
25. The Registrar-General of the Corporate Affairs Commission (CAC) shallwithin 14 days of the issuance of this Order ensure that all registrationprocesses at the CAC are fully automated through the CAC websitefrom the start of an application process to completion, including ensuring the availability of an online payment platform wherenecessary.

Effective Date of the Order
26. This Executive Order shall take effect immediately.
Dated this . . . . day of . . . . 2017.

Prof. Yemi Osinbajo, SAN, GCON
Acting President of the Federal Republic of Nigeria
***

By the turn of March 2019 and sequel to the above government directives, the Federal Government had set up a website by name https://businessmadeeasy.ng/ to consolidate and further the simplicity of (the harsh) business environment.

The following are important business laws guide or regulate commercial activities in Nigeria.

Business Laws in Nigeria
In discussing these laws, I want the reader to be aware that development of law or in fact the legal system is dynamic. Removal or/and promulgation of a law may occur from time to time, as the case may be. Thus, would-be-investor should endeavour to keep up to date in this respect. Similarly, I do

not claim that the laws that discussed below are exclusively all that you need to know.

Investment and Securities Act (ISA), 1999
The important provisions of the ISA are:
a. The law provides for the establishment of an Investmentand Securities Tribunal to adjudicate disputes arising fromthe operators of capital market and exchanges inNigeria.
b. The law establishes provision for the electronic transfer ofregistered shares.
c. ISA also allows for transmissionof shares by private companies with foreign participation, whichno longer requires the approval of Securities and Exchange Commission (SEC) concerning merger, acquisition or other forms ofbusiness synergy.
d. The ISA additionally made provision for the creation of anInvestor Protection Fund (IPF). This instrument aims to reimburse investors who suffer afinancial lossfrom the mismanagement of assets by a member of a stock exchange or by any member or director of the capital market.

ISA has other important provisions which would-be investor should take a good note.

Nigerian Investment Promotion Commission (NIPC) Act, 1995
NIPC Act formally brought into being, investment promotionagency of the Federal Government. The main duty, amongst others, of NIPC agency is registration of foreign investments in Nigeria. The predecessor of NIPC, the Nigerian Enterprises Promotion Act, 1989, is no longer in operation.

Companies and Allied Matters Act (CAMA), LFN 2004
This is the substantive law concerningwith registration and regulation of business in Nigeria: largely similar to the UK's Companies Act, 2006. CAMA regulates and registers both local and foreign company intending on doing business in Nigeria, notwithstanding if the alien business intends to stand alone or not. CAMA also takes notice of some exceptions and provisions of other applicable business laws.

Immigrations Matters and Permits
Prior to conducting business in Nigeria, notwithstanding the registration under CAMA as discussed above, the foreigner must obtain certain permits. The following are necessary.

1. A *business permit* is a legal requirement for the operation of a business in Nigeria with foreign investments: as a branch of either the alien company or subsidiary of a foreign business. The alien must obtain the permit from Ministry of Internal Affairs.

2. *Expatriate or Employment Quota* (Permanent or Temporary). This legal authorization is given by Ministry of Internal Affairs, to an alien to allow him or her to accepting a specific or designated job or employment in Nigeria.

3. *Resident Permit*. While visitors with necessary permits (visa) may enter and stay in Nigeria for up to 3 months, this tourist visa does not permit work or employment. However, a resident permit is required and sought from Immigration Department of Ministry of Internal Affairs, should the individual desires to stay beyond the aforementioned 3 months. Note

also the provision of expatriate and business permits.

4. *Combined Expatriate Residence Permit and Alien Card* or (CERPAC). Coming into force in 2002, CERPAC provides that aliens working orliving in Nigeria to carry CERPAC permit card. The objective of this structure is to make simple the process of acquiring both resident and alien permits.

Taxation

Taxation in Nigeria reflects what is obtainable in most countries: individual, property and business taxations. In effect, the three tiers (Federal, State and Local Government) of government collects different taxes as the law permits. There are two types of taxes in Nigeria: Direct and Indirect. Direct taxes consists of corporate income tax, personal income tax (PAYE for example), capital gains tax, petroleum profits tax; and other taxes coming under different names. On the other hands, indirect are value added tax (VAT) and custom duties on imports as well as excise duties; and finally stamp duties. The Federal Government collects corporation taxes and income taxes on its own employees such as the military personnel and civil servants. The State government's collects income taxes on employed residents within the specific state States also collect capital gain taxes of sale of property and assets. The local government collects (or suppose) to collect property taxes such as ground rents/tenement rates and other applicable local levies including such levies as building plan approval fees.

Education Tax

Registered Businesses in Nigeria pay Education tax of 2% of applicable profits in keeping with the stipulated termsof the

Education Tax Act No 7 of 1993. Foreign-owned companies are exemptfrom paying Educational Tax.

Tax Treaties

Nigeria has a number of tax agreements, which is referred to as "double taxation"treaties with some countries. Taxes are deductible and or payable by a company that makes profits on its business in Nigeria. Such profits are sent overseas by the foreign company. That is to say that if UK based company A does business in Nigeria and has a profit such a company is supposed to pay tax both in Nigeria and in the UK. Now, because company A has paid tax in Nigeria, the amount paid to Nigerian tax authorities will be subtracted from what company A will pay in the UK. These arrangements are reciprocal between the countries in the treaties. Some of these countries are France, the Netherlands, Belgium, and Canada. It is important to note that Nigerian governments and agencies will require from businesses, evidence of tax payment before they can do business with the government.

There are other taxes in Nigeria such as *Withholding Tax and Capital Gains Tax* amongst others, which are operational in Nigeria.

Labor Laws.

Nigeria is a member of International Labour Organization (ILO). Thus, as a member of ILO, Nigeria should be compliant with the rules and regulations or directives of the ILO. In fact, Nigeria has been a member of the ILO since 1960 and has ratified 40 international labour Conventions, according to ILO itself. Nevertheless, as we shall see later, the reality of labour structure especially as pertaining to employment of children and forced labour such as in trafficking of persons remain a huge task. Though the law exists to contain the offences of human trafficking, forced labour and employment of minor, the pragmatic execution and sustainability of such execution remain challenging (See the following legal enactments: *Trafficking In Persons (Prohibition) Law Enforcement And Administration Act, 2003 And Trafficking In Persons (Prohibition) Law Enforcement And Administration (Amendment) Act, 2005.* See also: *Trafficking in Persons (Prohibition), Enforcement and Administration Act, 2015 (Act No. 4 of 2015)*.

However, the substantive labour law in Nigeria is found in the Nigerian Labor Act. The Labor Act only covers employees or as the Labor Act expressed, "workers" engaged under a contract of manual labour or clerical work in private and public sectors. For more details, consult the Labor Act, 2004.

Still on labour issue, the truth of the matter is that compare to developed world, labour is cheap in Nigeria. The US dollar or Euro or British Sterling will go far in Nigeria in labour market. Just look at Nigerians on Linkedin (www.linkedin.com), you will be amazed to note that Nigerian are indeed well read and are very intelligent with diverse skills in manifold human endeavours. Most of these skills are within the frontiers of Nigeria while those in the diaspora are large repository of expertise. In spite of the expertise, perhaps for fear of repercussion, employees/workers (even also in public), do not often take proactive remedial steps when challenges appear. Very often, the boss must give directives as to what is necessary or what needs to be done. I found the latter perplexing.

Compulsory, Free Universal Basic Education Act, 2004 aimed at elimination of child labour and to offer protection of children and young personsthrough right of a child to compulsory, free universal basic education. However, the reality on the ground is pathetic and direct contradiction to what the laws says. Again, lawlessness and lack of determined execution of the law stems progress. Driven by poverty, children are employed when they should not be. In 2006, the number of child workers was estimated at about 15 million, according to *"Information Sheet - Child Labour in Nigeria,"* UNICEF. 2006.

In general, the following laws are relevant in Nigeria labour market and it is advisable for readers to take good note of them: The Factories Act, 2004, The Pensions Act, 2004, The Trade Disputes Act, 2004, The Trade Union Amended Act, 2005, The Employees Compensation Act, 2010, The National Minimum Wage Act, 2011 and The Pension Reform Act, 2014.

Business Forms
Whilst its open to individuals and entities or groups of persons on the way that they wish to conduct their businesses in Nigeria, from the legal perspective, foreign businesses seem certain to only be allowed if they are registered or incorporated bodies.

If the issue of alien is not applicable, then individuals or parties may choose to conduct their business affairs depending on what they intend to achieve. The business forms that are available in Nigeria are in general similar to what is obtainable in the UK or USA or elsewhere. That is to say, businesses can be *registered bodies*, *partnership* or be a*sole trader*. Of course, each of these forms have their pros and cons. A registered business (limited liability company, LLC) can sue and be sued. Such a body has a legal life of their own as distinct from the biological and legal life of their owner/shareholders. Unless, a partnership is registered as LLP (Limited Liability Partnership), conventional partnerships carry the risk of sole trader of unlimited liabilities. Sole traders have unlimited liabilities including the assets of the owner of the business being at risk of being used to settle debts and court cases.

That said, one may register business names at Corporate Affairs Commission office or online, even if the business is not yet in operation. Registration of a business name does not protect the name from being used by a registered business.

Understanding the Purchasing Power of Nigerian Consumers.
Though we have seen the various figures exemplifying the GDP, National Minimum Wage and the income per day of the average Nigeria in the poverty belt, this does not in any way illustrate the practical consuming power of Nigerians.

The detail is in the numbers: the huge number of Nigerians. This portion of the book is best illustrated by case studies of MTN or the whole mobile phone operators and Cowbell.

For a start, take a look at the magnificent arithmetic of trading with the poor masses. The poor cannot afford a big financial expenditure. Yet, they would like to consume water, chocolate drinks, food and also make phone calls like everyone else does.

Initially, big entrants, multinationals and conglomerates dream of big spenders. Yet, in a country, where majority are poor, this dream may soon become a vain illusion, leading as it so often does, to frustration and exiting the Nigerian market.

To overcome the frustration and to make big money, some companies including mobile phone providers have adopted a strategy to reach a large audience and to make unimaginable revenues and profits in the process. Assuming a chocolate drink company packages their powdery product in tins and sachets. While the tins of say 800grams content costs say N1000, the sachet of say 800 grams content costs N800 to take account of the tin which is an additional cost. Most families with say four children and individuals in Nigeria within the poverty spectrum are unable to afford this product even though they will like to buy this product to feed their family members. At best, if they do purchase this chocolate product, the product consumption may not last more than a week or two. By and large, this is an expensive product, yet consumers desire it.To overcome this barrier of want and being unable to meet the need, manufacturers have come up with a solution.

An item that would have otherwise been packaged at 800 grams and being sold in a tin or sachet can indeed be divided into bits of small packets. Such bits of small packets may be 50 grams each containing the *same quality* as the one for 800grams. The 50grams will now sell at a fraction of N1000. The cost may be N50 or even N100. Without doubt, most poor people in Nigeria will be able to afford N50-100 to be spent on a chocolate drink to satisfy the family at a given time rather than tying down N1000 for a month! The bits of consumption may be repeated as often as possible without causing significant harm to the family finances. The consequences are that: (1) The needs are met at an affordable price, (2) The frequency of consumption can be in control of the consumer without huge financial outlay (3) The nutritional needs of the individual and family are met. For the manufacturer and retailers, the product is (1) now a fast moving consumer item (2) able to reach as many millions as possible (3) revenue stream has expanded and increased considerably rather than being limited to a few huge spenders.

This key principle and strategy is seemingly what Cadbury, Nestle and Cowbell amongst others have employed to a considerable benefit: The recognition of the purchasing power of the poor. Even in the healthcare sector that is so capital intensive in setting up, some medical practitioners have found a way out of the barriers to entry: locate to the midst of the poor and disadvantaged population so as to take advantage of this key strategy. That is, sell to large masses at low prices. The downside though for healthcare is that quality may be diluted and this why physicians loath this strategy as employed by health maintenance organizations (HMO).

Another illustration involves water. Everyone needs potable water. As I mentioned before, potable water is scarce in Nigeria. Considering that typhoid and other food and water borne diseases are public health problems in Nigeria, some insightful business men and women sighted a huge business opportunity.

In my research, to produce "pure water" in sachet of 200-300 ml from a bore-hole in Nigeria, costs an average of N2-5 each. The retail price of "pure water" in sachet is N10. Millions of Nigerians drink this type of water in sachet every day. Assuming the margin is N3 taking account of logistic, tax and storage, then a producer that sells a million sachet a day goes home with N3million (about US$10,000) every day. This calculation does not take account of premium and big water producers such as Coca-Cola (producer of Eva) bottled water and Nestle to mention a few.

The mobile phone operators and mobile phone manufacturers have keyed into this spectacular strategy as earlier stated. Illustrating further still using communications: There are four major mobile phone service providers in Nigeria (Airtel, 9-Mobile, MTN and GLO). I subscribed to all four by reason of what will be discussed in the next chapter.

Each of these providers have the habit of sending unsolicited (often worthless) messages to subscribers. Except a subscriber takes the step to stop the messages, there is a huge risk of the providers deducting money, contrary to fiduciary duty, from the account of the subscriber. Here is the devil in the numbers and details. As at the last count, over 100 million Nigerians have access to mobile phones and internet. Now assuming MTN has 50million active subscribers who are receiving anunsolicited message costing N50 per day. MTN can send this message to 40 million subscribers in one day. Thus, without much effort, MTN will be making 50 x, 40 = N200 million per day on account of merely sending out uninvited SMS. That is approximately US$600,000 every single day without much effort than punching a few keys on its computers in a country where the majority earns less than $2 per day! Now repeat the same practice across all the networks! Multiply that by 365 days. This is just one stream of revenue for the service providers albeit a poorly regulated one and probably illegally generated revenue.

This same strategy is in use in the food industry even amongst petty traders and clothing merchants. Imagine cheap eggs and noodles that are consumed by millions of children and adults on a daily basis. There is power in numbers after all! Will this amount to exploitation of the poor? Remember though that Nigeria is a capitalist economy and the winners take all.

The banking industrial sector understood the phenomenal power of the Nigerian masses. Allegedly, there are fewer Nigerians with bank accounts as compared to the entire population. Yet, the bankers make huge profits on the back of the masses based on simple reasoning: deduct a fraction of Naira for each transaction and multiply that by millions of users! The resulting figures are staggering.

Now, this is not to say that, there is no market for premium consumers. Plenty of room exists for high end consumers. Ask the airlines. The Nigerian market is probably a free-for-all air market where airline operators especially, foreign operators, charge the most unreasonable fees for the same journey which a domestic airline owner will charge their customers. We should remember though that Nigeria is a savage, poorly regulated capitalist market where winners take it all. Allegedly, premium seats and first class at high seasons may not be available for booking with some airline operators. This throws into the debate this paradox: why should Nigeria be labelled a "poor" country? Some ostentatious behaviour of Nigerians at home and abroad contradicts this ironic label. Extend this strategy to education and the teeming school children that will need cheap books, decent classrooms and teachers! The resulting demographic and economic figures are just astounding!

The summary therefore is that parties intending on doing business in Nigeria, should consider their market segment carefully and act accordingly. Most certainly, the huge numbers are there and the masses are available to be served.

Beyond Fears

The Real Life Opportunities
As at the time of writing, Nigerians are poorly served in practically all areas of human needs and enterprise. Nigeria needs about 20 million homes. Clearly, providing such accommodation for the teeming masses is beyond any government. Lagos, one of the most expensive places to live on earth is in dire need of lots of cheap homes.For the cheap homes to happen though, the financial system, the credit and mortgage industry will require an overhaul; root and branch. There lay other set opportunities within *housing:* credit rating agencies accessible by the masses, access to mortgages and good monitoring systems. The towns and villages need areas of preservation, exclusivity, and dedicated housing development. Now, chaos and random housing appear to prevail at the moment. Business opportunity anyone?

Communication has indeed improved in Nigeria compared to the period when only 500,000 linesexisted before the dawn of mobile phone operators. Internet broadband bandwidth is still ancient and perhaps one of the slowest in the world. Address and access to home addresses along with postage system are dysfunctional and chaotic. The postal system is ancient and essentially close to being overlooked by the masses. Can anyone see a business opportunity to fix thechaotic system that will make the link between communication, logistics, tracking and tracing of people, goods as well as businesses seamless for a modern era?

Energy. Apart from political leadership, perhaps nothing annoys Nigerians more than the energy deficit. Can anyone provide the teeming Nigerians with cheap, mass-produced power source for every home and business in the land? With 12-hour daily sun energy supply in an equatorial region, with massive open end to windy Atlantic ocean: Can a deep minded business entity tap into the vast landscape and provide the nation of Nigeria of nearly 200 million people, with accessible, available and affordable solar or other alternative uninterrupted power? The prospect is open and awaiting takers.

Education Nigeria is a hungry nation when it comes to qualitative education. Many prospective students are disappointed yearly for not getting into their desirable course and institutions at all levels of education. This is notwithstanding the liberalization of the educational system and the establishment of many private schools at all levels. Many Nigerians go abroad due to the previously mentioned frustrations. Can overseas universities locate satellite or overseas branches in Nigeria to offer good quality education? The birth rate of Nigerians is high. The current educational system is obviously not coping.

Agriculture: Whilst there has been considerable improvement and re-energization of the agricultural sector relative to when the sector was abandoned to the chase of petroleum in the 1970s to 1990s, a lot still needs to be done. Food storage remains a challenge. Seamless transportation, processing and packaging are still of ancient methods. Improvement in taste, resistance to infection, better methodology of farming and continuing research by wide variety of institutions are continuing voids. When will Nigerian oranges that perish in such large quantities be processed into the likes of *"100% pure orange juice with bits"* in the manner of "Tropicana Orange Juice" for example? The same question can be asked of hundreds of diverse fruit, nuts, seeds and animal produce that are presently in Nigeria but going to waste because of lack of good processing and storage.

Transport: Well-industrialized, organized, land and sea transportation systems are forlorn hopes. In the last few years, the government has put in place skeletal transportation systems linking very few towns and cities. Such efforts are insignificant in comparison to massive transportation infrastructure and network systems of developed economies such as China. Land and Sea transport systems, be it for commuting or for haulage still remain largely rudimentary, not to mention transport for leisure and tourism. Basic and luxury ferries for practical purposes is at zero level, not existing at all and neither are Speed trains.

For air transport, a lot still needs to be done but local airlines require serious competition as much as airports are yearning for improvements to meet international standards. I hope the reader can sense some business opportunities here. Local manufacturing rather than assembling of vehicle parts is scarce. Does that sound like an opportunity?

Healthcare: An overhaul of the healthcare sector is required but may not happen fast. The opportunities in healthcare are huge in secondary and tertiary areas. Credible, accessible, affordable health institutions of international repute with up-to-date standards in a conducive environment will rescue Nigerians from spending US$1billion annually on medical tourism. Medical research is poor and few see reason to go into research. Reward may not be so forthcoming in view of the pressure on individuals to meet personal financial needs.

Manufacturing in healthcare sector provides considerable opportunities as almost all hardware equipment that physicians require which are presently all imported into the country. Few basic medicines are locally made in Nigeria. The market is flooded with unverified preparations from

China and India. The making of complex precision medical devices, manufacturing of important medications that are out of patents are rare in Nigeria. Yet Nigeria has many natural resources to meet its needs: from petroleum products to earth minerals. Consumables such as gloves are imported yet Nigeria has many human and materials resources to make rubber gloves. The opportunities are incredibly large. Are you still unsure what business opportunity you may undertake in Nigeria? Think again!

Retail. Nigeria's retail market is currently in favour of the bold. Few outlets meet international standards: *Spar* and *Shoprite.* Shoprite is only one dominant force that actually sees 700 malls in Nigeria, according to the owner. Nigeria needs competition in malls of high quality and international standards. Can take the risk, but won't take the risk? Is that you?

Other Service Industries that you may consider are: Law and legal professions need vibrancy, innovation and competition. There are many sectors of law that are not addressed in Nigeria. Hotels and the hospitality industry have seen some improvement in major cities such as Lagos and Abuja. However, tourism does not get a significant mention in the national economy. In the non-service sector, prospecting for earth minerals and manufacturing in general are worth considering.

Practical Steps Requiredin Starting and Running a Business in Nigeria
At the beginning of this chapter, you read a reproduction of the Executive Order by the Presidency. Obviously, the Nigerian Government recognizes the immense difficulties in doing business in Nigeria. Entry barriers are high for new

entrants and maintaining an existing business is wrought with man-made challenges: bureaucratic bottlenecks, corruption, attitudinal issues of public servants, logistics, communication barriers, security challenges are some but not exhaustive problems. For some of these reasons the Federal Government made the Executive Order to ease the business climate.

Anyone, regardless of your status, whether alien or citizen contemplating doing business in Nigeria, should consider the contents of this book as well as the outline below. I run a business and live in Nigeria: so my recommendations come from practical experiences. I do not warrant that I have covered all grounds. This is so because new laws emerge frequently and human behavior, in addition to dynamic political-economic forces, undergoes change daily.

1. Register the business (For profit or not for profit business) with CAC (Corporate Affairs Commission). The recent Executive Order of the Presidency has made registration simple. Registration can now be done online as opposed to previous onerous process of going to Abuja or employing a third party such as a lawyer to do the registration at an exorbitant fee. If you are not sure that you have the ability or understanding or you do not have the time to do the registration by yourself, simply consider using a third party, most advisably in the person of a lawyer. The lawyer's fees in the days before the Executive order or when lawyers had to work through third parties themselves, could range from anything up to N70,000 (US$200). Any amount exceeding N100, 000 is probably exploitative. I have witnessed a figure of N1m (approximately US$3000) being quoted for business registrationthough. Do your research and

carry out appropriate legwork. Remember that Nigeria is a savage capitalist country: anything goes. If you are ignorant, you may be exploited. In Nigeria, lawyers practice as an advocate, solicitor, or both. No specific demarcation really exists between solicitor and advocate. The current web address of the CAC is http://new.cac.gov.ng/home/. Alternatively, simply "Google" (that is use online search engine) to search for "business registration with CAC in Nigeria." Then follow the appropriate search results of your choice. The requirements for registration have been simplified. Note that for aliens, there are additional requirements earlier explained in the previous chapter.

2. For business name registration, the procedure is similar to registration of a business. The requirements for business registration are even simpler. The CAC still deals with business name registration.

3. If you choose to do business as a sole trader, you should know the risks and benefits. For you to trade solely, it implies, you are a Nigerian or you have satisfied the law in this regards.

4. In case you decide on partnership as your preferred form of doing business in Nigeria, kindly consider that the Partnership Act of the UnitedKingdom is still applicable in Nigeria though Lagos State seems to have a version of their own. It is advisable, that in all cases and in whatever form the partnership may be, (such as between individuals or between registered businesses or individuals and registered businesses) always have anauthentically written and validly executed agreement in place. Nigeria has a

strong history of orality. Never accept the persuasion that there will be no trouble because you belong to the same family, you are husband and wife, you attend the same church or that you are friends. Oral agreement may not suffice in Nigeria.

5. Insurance: To protect your business, you need insurance. Take a good cover with a fair premium. The state of the insurance industry in Nigeria seems to have improved with the advent of *National Insurance Commission Act of 1997 and the Insurance Act of 2003*. Nonetheless, the uptake of insurance against losses still lags behind in Nigeria. As at October 2017, there were only 28 Insurance Companies providing general insurance. There were only 14 insurance companies providing life insurances. Those providing professional liabilities insurances are probably fewer in number. These insurances are distinct and should not be confused with the Health Management Organization (HMO or "insurance") though the likes of AXA-Mansard crisscross the health and life insurance platforms. For more on the regulation of Insurance Industry in Nigeria, readers should contact National Insurance Commission. (www.naicom.gov.ng).

6. Agreement/Contract: Resolution of disputes require the rule of law and speedy dispensation of justice. For International or alien businesses operating in Nigeria, especially if the agreement involves any arm or agency of the government at any level, consider the resolution of dispute to be in a country with strict rule of law such as the United Kingdom or the United States of America or other European Union

countries. State this condition in the contract where the dispute resolution will be based. Litigation can be frustrating in Nigeria and resolution may take forever never mind the alleged corruption of judges. If the agreement is operative locally within Nigeria, consider using alternative dispute resolution and an arbitration panel as the final arbiter. Whilst going to court may be an option, it may not be the best strategic legal and economic decision. Remember that Nigerians are deeply religious. Persuasion to forgive wrongs is common and seeking restitution for damages could be frowned at. If you do intend to seek damages, be bold and have credible evidence available.

7. Banking: You will need multiple bank accounts. Choose any bank of your choice. There are many banks in Nigeria that are operating at international levels. Having a single bank account is a sure path to disappointment and frustrations. These banks issue business and personal debit cards and they are accepted internationally and online. Caution: These cards may be rejected both online and offline. Therefore, prepare for an alternative source of funding your shopping with PayPal (www.paypal.com) as an alternative. PayPal operates in Nigeria. You are allowed to transfer money out of Nigeria from your PayPal account in Nigeria but not permitted to transfer money into your PayPal account from any other source other than your bank account that is domiciled in Nigeria. One is not certain if as at the time of writing PayPal could be used as an online fund merchant for Nigerian businesses. There are locally developed mechanisms or platforms (In-

terswitch) that workwith the banks, and facilitate online commerce. Mobile banking in Nigeria is fantastically better than I have seen anywhere else in the world. It works seamlessly. Banking apps are also available for mobile phones but their use and functionality depends on the working of the mobile phones service providers. If there is a down time, which is not uncommon, with mobile phone service providers, your banking app may not work accordingly. ATMs (automatic teller machines) are available widely in major towns and cities and interbank arrangements allows for use of one ATM belonging to another bank. The use of another bank's ATM may be subject to a small fee surcharge usually from the third transaction. The debit card from one issuer may fail due to communication and infrastructural problems. Therefore, it is safe and advisable to always carry multiple bankcards everywhere you go. If one bankcard does not work, another will. For security reasons, carrying a lot ofphysical cash, be it local or foreign currency is not advisable. If you are seen with a large amount of cash, especially foreign currency, you may be robbed, detained or both by police or bandits. The cash may be lost by any other means. That said, a little cash for emergency use that is just enough to sustain you safely should always be with you or within your reach.

8. Business location: Your location will depend on your type of business and you will need to do a lot of research and legwork on this and physically view various places before deciding on location or localization of your business. You may consider security,

transport, ease of communication, business that operates like yours, access to market and raw materials, etcetera.

9. Communication, Internet: Just as for banking, you will need multiple phone lines from different providers. In case one line or provider fails, you can easily switch to another without any disruptions to your business. The mobile phone providers are the main internet providers though there are some standalone internet/data providers. Vodacom provides data. You may also obtain a permit for your own exclusive satellite internet beaming.

10. Mass Media: There are many newspapers in Nigeria such as the Guardian, Thisday, BusinessDay, The Nation, Punch, Daily Trust. Most if not all are online as well. Television and radio stations are equally numerous. Some are owned by the public and others by private enterprises. There are international "cable" or satellite televisions such as DSTV and Startimes amongst others. These satellite or "cable" television providers broadcast from international stations, especially DSTV.

11. Shopping: Shoprite is a standard mall that has outlets all across Nigeria. Spar is a supermarket of international origins too. There are smaller ones that provide the same services. Retailers of food and other items are common on main streets in major cities. Market days are regular in countryside villages and towns. Most countryside markets operate once a week. Haggling is the norm and permitted. Food is often fresh and natural though may occa-

sionally be stale if not well preserved by the seller. Internet shopping is open to everyone. There are local players like Jumia and Konga and international outlets such as EBay (ebay.com or ebay.co.uk) and (www.amazon.comor www.amazon.co.uk) who ship directly to Nigeria for most purchases. A warning is required: debit cards issued in Nigeria are sometimes rejected by online shops. I have had difficulties using my Visa/Mastercard issued by banks in Nigeria. Bankcards issued by overseas banks as in the United Kingdom orthe USA may become readily helpful when shopping online.

12. Healthcare. The choice is yours depending on your pocket depth and your location. In big cities, there are good private health institutions. Do not expect International standards although some private institutions are trying their very best irrespective of their sizes. You can inspect before use. You may also act based on recommendation of locals combined with your personal judgment. In the case of an emergency, how a healthcare provider looks is immaterial. Use whatever is available for the emergency then proceed to a more refined care center once you are stable. There are tertiary centers by government and private institutions especially in big cities. The trouble with government health facilities are personnel. They may be on industrial dispute and down tools for a long time. The government facilities may not be to your taste. Therefore good, credible and diligent though pricey private practitioners become the next best option. There are also local health maintenance organizations (HMO). Long term

international health insurance can be obtained from international players such as AXA-Mansard (Nigeria) or BMI Healthcare(UK) or via any other recognized health insurance providers. The advantage of the International insurance or travel insurance as the case may be, is that victims can be transferred overseas for further care if required. Depending on the premium being paid to the HMO, a local HMO can fund extensive healthcare. It is strongly advisable that if you fall ill, you request for the diagnosis from the people that are caring for you. Do a bit of research online too regarding your illness. Ask for details of your medication. If surgery is planned, ask for the reason. If you can afford it, seek a second opinion for your treatment. If you are not sure of your progress, seek a transfer to where you know or a place you are comfortable with. Be feisty, humble, alert and vigilant as to your care. Always ask questions on your treatment and progress. Upon discharge, ask that a medical report on your treatment be given to you.

13. Land and Housing: As it operates everywhere in the world, where you live defines you: so do some research. Sedate or tranquil areas are in GRA (Government Reserved Areas) and new estates that are developed privately. All these come at a premium fees for good reasons: security and maintenance of the estates. Land matters is complex in Nigeria but in general, all land is subject to The Land Use Act that was enacted by the Federal Government in the 70s. All States have a varied version to meet their local needs. Land can be "Government Land" which has been acquired for public use. Land own-

ership may also rest with family members. Government may acquire land from family members or any member of the public. Therefore, if you are looking for land, these are the two parties to acquire land from. Such land may have been passed on from hand to hand. In the countryside and in cities, the kings or emirs or obis or obas, may help acquire land via negotiations with family members or whoever may be the owner of the land. Therefore, the third parties that sell land are those that have acquired the land from the government or family members. Estate agents may help search out available land for acquisition. Some estate agents are online and they appear well presented. So many things are secretive in Nigeria. Land or housing transactions may not be so obvious or be made public for all to see. Spouses (especially in polygamous homes) and "enemies" may allegedly come after the vendor of theland for a share of the money. Alternatively, the whole land sale may degenerate into a family or local feud. A single land parcel may be sold to several parties simultaneously by the alleged vendor(s): leading as it often does to fraud, deception and violence. Therefore, you should get your land from an authentic source, after having carried out extensive research to authenticate the ownership using credible lawyers, taking photos/videos of the land and land sellers and registering the land that is sold withthe respective government agency. Land search can also be done at government Land Registry. Each state has one of such. Never buy property or land in cash. Never part with money without genuine and verified land ownership; along with good contract and credible documentation for the land.

Keep your land documents in an impenetrably safe place (bank, vault and so forth).

14. Schools: Schools are everywhere. Ownership is equally diverse. Owners may be religious, charity, government or private individuals. The quality is diverse. Private schools hardly ever go on strike. Go on a personal visit and collect information on each school (fees, reputation, exam scores). Compare data. As for healthcare, so for schools. All schools are supposed to be registered and monitored by respective local and state government authorities. Federal Schools are monitored by the Federal Ministry of Education and are open to all Nigerian residents. Quality you remember, is in the eye of the beholder. Do your research and legwork before making a decision. Most, if not all good schools have online presence.

Targeting Success through Diversification of Product Lines:
Nigeria is a unique country in many respects. Economic theories and practices that work in advanced economies may not work in Nigeria. For example, the Keynesian inverse economic relationship between inflation and unemployment does not hold in Nigeria. Both inflation and unemployment run high pari-pasu. Another example: having a single functional product such as a single bank account, single mobile phone and so forth is tantamount to self-suffocation. Those services may fail at any time. So as not to be "left in the wilderness" without support, Nigerians have adapted to having multiple consumer products. Many Nigerians have multiple jobs or businesses to improve personal incomes. The idea is that should one debit card fail for example or a sim card or even a car fail to work, another will. The "another" must

always be available for use. This practice applies to multiple energy sources too, which gives rise to the use of generators, solar-inverters and the national grid all in one property.

Thus, businesses that intend to survive Nigeria should diversify widely for it is dangerous to stick to a single product line as is the practice elsewhere in the world. Even within the same industrial sector such as healthcare, aclinical practitioner should diversify and they often do, into say clinical practice, pharmacy retail and medical equipment supply. Businesses that intend to survive the Nigerian economy may also cross multiple industrial sectors as Dangote Group of Companies has done with building matrials, oil and gas as well as the food industry. Coscaharis also diversified into automobile and healthcare equipment supply, not to forget the proprietors of Zenith Bank and Glo Mobile who are also into oil and gas. To hold on to a single product line is a risky endeavour in Nigeria.

Chapter 4.
Cautions, Pitfalls and Warnings
Trust, Utilities, Will and Trust for Legacy Preservation, Personality Requirements, Material Requirements for Would-be Nigerian Resident.

"My one purpose in life is to serve as a warning to others."
---Jamie Zawinski

In this concluding chapter, I will deal with some issues that often thrust fears into Nigerians, would be Nigerian residents and prospective alien businesses. Some of these matters are at the foundation of what has created a bad impression of Nigeria. Further, by heeding to the warnings and cautions that are contained in this discourse, you can avoid the dangers and be able to navigate the Nigerian environment safely.

Trust: If trust were to be personified into a real human being, one can confidently say that trust died a tragic death a long time ago in Nigeria. The simple truth is, trust no one: not your friends, strangers, co-workers, public servants nor family members. I have been betrayed by family members. I have been let down, plotted against and blackmailed by supposed friends colluding with strangers. What could have been the target of all the treachery? The simple answer is money, extortion and a callous attempt at economic extraction for personal gain. Nigerians revel in orality and loathe anything that needs to be written or signed. Therefore, never allow yourself to be carried away by sugar-coated tongues, false promises and religious-tainted fraudulent reassurances whose ends are deception and economic exploitation. The issue of trust cannot be over-emphasized. Never trust anyone in Nigeria with information or material that may have a monetary value. Never rely on family members to rescue or support you especially if you are wealthy or thrifty. They may just be waiting for your demise so that the battle for your estate may begin.

There are three shades of advisers in Nigeria and you won't be short of advisers. Some operate in penumbra of darkness, some are in pitch darkness and some are in bright light: all giving advice depending on the depth of their knowledge, exposure and understanding of the specific issue at hand. One thing is sure, you are never going to be short of advisers whatever your mission is and wherever you are even if the advice is based on falsehood, guesswork, self-gain, half-truths, incompetence, deception, manipulation or and an attempt at your exploitation. This scenario is so, because of the total lack of official transparency at all levels, poor regulatory framework of service and product providers, individual struggle for survival, and hard-to get facts of the matter. The genuine advisers operating in bright light are hard to come by but do exist and are God-sent when you get them. One must listen carefully, pretend to accept all advice: so as not to offend advisers and not to lose the real angel of truth and helpers when they come. To circumvent the unfortunate scenario of being misled and or exploited, search for the required facts everywhere, confirm and authenticate each given word and written document. Do not take anything on face value. Do not willingly and naively part with money. Nothing ever comes easy in life. The easier the route or promises, the more likely that the end may be bitter. Seek advice and counsel independently before taking action. The law is weak here and restitution may never come.

Public Utilities Services: You rely on public utilities and services at your risk and peril. Public water, power supply, healthcare, security and rescue. If you happen to be a landlord, ensure you have your own water supply, often via boreholes that is bored into a small space within your compound. Except for desalination, the water from the earth core is good for drinking. Borehole should be far away from cesspit/septic tanks. From time to time, obtain bottled water to supplement the borehole water if you prefer.

Electricity or public power supply is a mess. You need your own energy source. Solar panels with inverter batteries will provide an easy solution at a cost. You will need a back-up generator. With these two, you may live comfortably within your means anywhere in Nigeria. The amount of energy you need depends on what you use the energy for. Businesses will require a greater supply. Private homes with refrigerators and air-conditioners will require bigger systems. Lesser home infrastructure needs less energy generation. If the national grid or public supply is available, then it helps to compliment your energy consumption. Never rely on public energy as your primary energy source. You need to remain vigilant day and night as to the functionality of all your systems. You may not like the consequences of failure. Get your systems tested to ensure that the infrastructure works: even in the presence of an engineer that may have just repaired or serviced the systems. Learn to get your hands dirty too except if you are rich and have loads of maids at your disposal. You may need the experience in the days of adversity.

Safety: Rescuefrom dangerous situations or during accidents is not guaranteed. This is the hard truth: You may die or get lost without ever being found. Being "lost" may be due to kidnapping, self-wandering leading to disorientation, or due to some misfortune. Avoid being in such circumstances as much as you can. Travel less except if your voyage is necessary. Alternatively, you may have your own escort motorcade with ambulance if you can afford one. In my opinion, this motorcade and escorts are the privileges or preserves of governors and high government officials. Violence or threat of it along with accidents on the one hand and illness especially epidemic on the other hand constitute what can cause residents in Nigeria immediate significant apprehension.

Healthcare: Of illness, rampant infection is of concern. Food borne infection such as typhoid and poisoning bacteria or their toxins are major threats. Malaria causing mosquitoes are ubiquitous. Sanitation is poor as is trust in public "potable" water. The solution is in one's hand. Only trust (see discussion of trust above) few good names of water and food sources or firmly decide not to eat beyond your home if domestic food handlers and the raw food are themselves free of infection. Delay in seeking quality health care can be deadly. Life is far too cheap here. Personally, when I travel out of my comfort zone, I carry along essential medication everywhere that I go: including anti-malarial drugs, anti-typhoid drugs, anti-allergy drugs, antibacterial drugs, antiviral medication, analgesics, plasters, wound cleaners and antiseptics. You may need to have a good healthcare insurance or have a retinue of rescuers in case of an emergency.

Critical Material Requirements For Living in Nigeria.
People born and bred in Nigeria are in some ways used to the challenges of their environment: frustrating as it may seem. Residents tend to adapt or give up trying. Individuals who have adapted well and are successful are highly unlike-

ly to desire leaving Nigeria except perhaps for investment expansion or for pleasure. New persons who are visiting or intending to reside in Nigeria could easily perceive Nigeria as unlivable. To live in Nigeria to a good degree of comfort, some fundamental material possessions are required. The need for these materials apply to all irrespective of if one is born or reared in Nigeria or not. The first and most important of them all is housing. Become a landlord whatever it takes except if you are planning a short stay. Even a short stay but one that you may visit the country frequently demands that one should endeavor to become a landlord. Being the owner of the property that one resides in has many advantages. You are free from the harassment of landlords who may lack any trace of decency. Landlords may make life unbearable for tenants. In addition, you are a king in your own home and you feel secure whatever may be happening elsewhere. One is not oblivious to the fact that Nigeria requires 20million housing units and not everyone could become a landlord in a country where mortgage lending is hellish, inaccessible and unaffordable to most. For this reason, Nigerians could build any structure in any space possibly available.

Anyone with the privilege of advanced planning or with the financial resources, should take heed to this housing advice. It is not enough to have a house or a home located just anywhere. Risk of invasion of privacy, political insurrection, religious disturbance and incredible noise pollution could drive one crazy if one is unfortunate to live in bad neighborhood.

Thus, in seeking one's accommodation, I will advise that prospective residents seek local advice and personally pay a visit to potential areas they are interested in. At a cost, residing in GRA (Government Reserved Areas) and private estates located away from markets and crowds are advisable. Alternatively, an exclusive home in the countryside with definite wide areas of personal space and security is in order. Consider access to schools, ease of access to other areas of town and cities, access to local shops and a good distance away from any religious institution. Avoid areas that are prone to stampede. The closer ones place of residence is to ones work, the better. This means less travel and less risk to your life.

Transport. With housing secured, the next important item is how to navigate the nooks and corners of your environment. Remember though that except for Google Map, there is no conventional common navigational tool (navigator) in Nigeria. Most roads are chaotic and streets may not be motorable. Public transport may not be to your taste. If advanced preparation is possible or personal finances permit, get at least two cars. You will need them. Nigerians are fully aware that to function at ones optimum, one needs at least two cars, two jobs (at least two sources of income), one God but two religions, two mobile phone providers, two bank accounts, two homes and if possible even two spouses hence prevalence of polygamyin Nigeria despite the high risk of infections! Your life is at risk with a reliance on a single essential functional item! Always have a Plan B for any arrangement. Human beings may disappoint and the system or infrastructure may fail without notice.

Income. Lazy people cannot survive Nigeria.It is a great misfortune for one: to be physically, economically and mentally disabled in Nigeria. Nigeria favours the strong and the determined. You need a regular income whatever that income may be. There is a common saying in Nigeria that whatever you are selling, you will find a buyer for it. Engage in a productive effort, any effort you choose. There is no limitation in Nigeria (the sky is not a limitation in Nigeria) though it is advisable to attempt to comply with the law. One may so easily experience the cruelty in Nigeria if living without money or you have no close helper/handler. The saying that living in Nigeria is not for the faint-hearted is not a hyperbole. The first timer to the country may experience cultureshock. In a country without any genuine safety net or social benefit or support of any kind, the mantra of living in the country is survival of the fittest, which comes with all the attendant brutalities and harshness that are found in the animal kingdom. If you are lucky, you may be helped by God-fearing and bold Nigerians. Nigerians have come to realise that kindness comes at a cost and has its limitations. Armed robbers and kidnappers who pretend to need help and have indeed been helped by kind-hearted persons but then turned around to harm their helpers are well rehearsed and now very common scenarios in Nigeria.

Personality Requirement to Live in Nigeria. Nigerians have a well-rehearsed axiom: If you can survive in Nigeria, you can survive anywhere. This saying is a mathematical truism. But how? Determination and teflon resilience is the key. Come rain or sunshine.Grit andruggedness are required. I am often perplexed as to why Nigerians hold so much to life. Religion may play a part but probably. Hope of a better tomorrow, as reiterated by religious doctrines makesNigerians determined to reach the promised land of good life and wealth. All you need is endurance to see you through your suffering.To survive in Nigeria, you need hope, determination, sheer hard work, personal sacrifices and focus. Few are thieves in Nigeria, pilfering public funds or private enterprise money for their own benefit. The rest of the masses are hard working.

If one is blessed with the privilege of foresight and advanced planning, all of the problems that are prevalent in Nigeria can be circumvented. In similar manner, with a good family fortune or one being fortunate to come to wealth early, with application of wisdom and due diligence, all of the challenges that are pointed out in this book can be minimized.

Nigeria is no hell but it is no heaven either.

Another important element that is required to navigate the Nigerian environment is to not only not to trust anyone, but also to be physically present in all situations. Lies and manipulation abound. If you have a project or business or work of any kind, be physically present to supervise it ensuring the execution of the work or project is according to your desired specification. Staying a long distance away from the point of project or relying on anyone is living dangerously. Fathers/parents can undo their children. Siblings kill each other and friends easily betray one another for material and financial gain. If these close relationships can be so treacherous to one another: how much more strangers and people in authority?

Will and Testament: Finally, it is pertinent to remember that dead people do not and cannot talk in self-defense. Your property is at risk of being squandered or left to decay if you do not have a credible and valid unambiguous record of how your legacy should be maintained. An unambiguous record, simply means a will and testament in writing and advisably also with a video recording of you reciting the will and testament. Since Nigerians may not be so reliable except a few, seek the good ones to guard your legacy. Institutions such as banks may be better as being guardians but they are still manned by human beings, who are still Nigerians. Vigilance is still required.

The ultimate question now is, with all the problems and challenges that seem so entrenched in Nigeria: is the gain worth the risk? Otherwise stated, is the value to be gained worth the risks? The answer is simple: wherever there is a high yield, there is certainly a high risk. The country may not be for the faint-hearted at first sight, but as the motto of the British SAS (Special Air Service) says, he who dares wins.

In sum, provided you keep within the ambit of the law, stay within your reasonable personal limits, have a penchant for identifying danger and danger zones and knowing when to pull back from a mission, you may give Nigeria a go. For businesspersons, the requirements are the same as it is in any country: sound strategy, endurance, focus, working with and valuing people, good financial management and never stray away from the law. With all these in mind, Nigeria surely is it, and as the economists will say, the end justifies the means.

Practical Survival Tips:
For those readers who are perhaps too busy to read this book at a go, I have provided the following summary points. The following practical tips are not intended to be in a particular order of importance. They are not exclusive either.

1. Get a home in a safe place located in a calm area devoid of religious, political and economic stampede: being easily

accessible relative to your work place and shopping is a top priority.

2. Get a generator and an inverter to supply you needed energy.

3. Get a good water supply, preferably a borehole and bottled water.

4. Get to arrange an income system be it be a personal business or an employment.

5. Get vehicle that will be conveying you for the long term or rely on the likes of Uber/Taxify for the short term. The alternative is the inconvenient but available public transport.

6. While your housemaid/helper/employees may be helpful, never trust them. However, keep your lack of trust to yourself and watch.

7. Always write your instructions down for the maid/helper and employees. Attention deficit is common here in both adults and children. Denial of faults committed is also rampant. Taking personal responsibility for negligence and faults are rare. Rather, a third party, often unseen animate or inanimate objects are often blamed. It may go thus: Question: "why did you fail to remove the clothes from the clothing line outside and you allowed the rain to fall on them?" Answer: "The sun set too late and the rain followed shortly after." Another example: "why did you fail to switch off the fan?" Answer:' "I didn't know the power supplier will restore power so soon." The President of the Country is often blamed for personal failings even when such failings are due to personal negligence or laziness.

8. Keep records (written records including texts, videos, photos and contracts). Denials, falsification with a view to duplication and manipulation are rife here. Keep them in duplicates if they are important. Keep your important documents secure in separate places.

9. Trust no one except perhaps a very few.

10. Avoid eating outside the home except from trusted sources. But never show your host that you are arrogant. Collect the food for further processing. Night wandering is risky too.

11. Avoid greed and lure of easy money or contract. It may lead to death or severe harm. Say No. Escape. Just never, get involved and avoid obstructing others that are bent on committing fraud. Just find a way that your name may not be tarnished.

12. If someone gives you a contract or does some kind gesture to you, you should make a "return" too. Pay to Caesar what is Caesar's. Do so speedily: often monetary. Nothing goes for nothing here. Do not do so in an embarrassing manner either. Be discreet in humble submission, with a thankful heart, even amongst friends.

13. Keep cheques, personal information, wills/testament, debit/credit cards safe and secure always. Keep less cash at home.

14. Never argue with an armed person: be it an official as police or a person in civilian attire. Resolve the issue and leave safely.

15. Bribe is common. Follow your conscience or abandon the value that is being chased by you. If your life is at risk, give the bribe and leave safely especially if the "enforcer" carries an object such as a knife or gun to do harm or intend on doing you harm.

16. Be generous to people around you and especially to the less privileged while ensuring that you don't come to harm at the same time or later. Kindness could breed cruelty towards a kind person here A kind person could be perceived as weak.

17. Have multiple bank accounts, multiple phones and sim cards, multiple internet providers, at least two cars and multiple sources of income.

18. Always make an alternate arrangement or Plan B for anything and everything.

19. Time keeping is never a virtue here. Adapt accordingly.

20. Flow with the crowd or individuals that seek to pray with you even if you do not or will never belong to such a party's beliefs.

21. Be practical and diligent in everything. Be physical. Be present and be vigilant in every sense. Never rely on assurances. "Go there" unannounced and see things for yourself or delegate to a trusted proxy. Investigate all information and ascertain the truth. Deception is common here.

In summary, the lack of rule of law---this breeds injustice, lawlessness, arbitrariness, impunity, god-fatherism---with cruelty of law enforcement in addition to onerous personal material requirement to survive such as housing: do make living in Nigeria very perilous. Furthermore, lack of financial credit systems, weak healthcare system and lack of comprehensive official social support make living in Nigeria a high-risk enterprise.

On the other hand, a careful navigation of the Nigerian system with the knowledge and lure that business environment is almost virgin: with expansive consumer base is irresistible. Similarly, understanding the diverse culture, complying with the law and doing a lot of self-help infrastructural/utility works, focusing on one's mission, being vigilant against all forms of abuses and even being hypervigilant against threat to personal security make living in Nigeria a worthwhile exercise. Good luck!

Appendix:

Major Regulators and Government Agencies at the Federal Level in Nigeria are listed below. The import of this list is to help individuals and intending businesses to channel their search at the appropriate quarters. All of these or most have internet presence according to their names. As indicated in the main book, physical personal presence is still preferred than any other way of communicating with these agencies.

Agriculture
Cocoa Research Institute of Nigeria, (CRIN)
National Agricultural Extension, Research and Liaison Services (NAERLS)
National Veterinary Research Institute (NVRI)
Nigerian Agricultural Insurance Corporation (NAIC)
National Root Crops Research Institute (NCRI)
Agricultural Research Council of Nigeria
Nigerian Institute for Oceanography and Marine Research
Nigerian Institute for Oil Palm Research (NIFOR)
Nigeria Agricultural Quarantine Service (NAQS)
National Horticultural Research Institute (NIHORT)

Aviation
Federal Airports Authority of Nigeria (FAAN)
Nigerian Airspace Management Agency (NAMA)
Nigerian Civil Aviation Authority (NCAA)
Accident Investigation Bureau (AIB)
Nigerian Meteorological Agency (NIMET)
Nigerian College of Aviation Technology (NCAT)

Communications
National Information Technology Development Agency (NITDA)
Nigeria Communications Satellite Limited (NIGCOMSAT)
Nigerian Broadcasting Commission (NBC)
Nigerian Communications Commission (NCC)
Nigerian Postal Service (NIPOST)
National Frequency Management Council

Economy
Asset Management Corporation of Nigeria (AMCON)
Budget Office of the Federation (BOF)
Bureau of Public Enterprises (BPE)
Bureau of Public Procurement (BPP)
Central Bank of Nigeria (CBN)
Corporate Affairs Commission (CAC)
Debt Management Office (DMO)
Federal Inland Revenue Service (FIRS)
Federal Mortgage Bank of Nigeria (FMBN)
Infrastructure Concession Regulatory Commission (ICRC)
National Bureau of Statistics (NBS)
National Council on Privatisation (NCP)
National Insurance Commission (NAICOM)
National Pension Commission PenCom (PenCom)
National Planning Commission (NPC)
National Sugar Development Council (NSDC)
Niger Delta Development Commission (NDDC)
Nigeria Customs Service (NCS)
Nigeria Deposit Insurance Corporation (NDIC)
Nigeria Investment Promotion Commission (NIPC)
Nigerian Export - Import Bank (NEXIM Bank)
Nigerian Export Promotion Council (NEPC)
Nigeria Export Processing Zones Authority (NEPZA)

Securities and Exchange Commission (SEC)
Standards Organisation of Nigeria (SON)
Small and Medium Enterprise Development Agency of Nigeria (SMEDAN)

Education
Joint Admissions and Matriculation Board (JAMB)
National Examination Council (NECO)
National Open University of Nigeria (NOUN)
National Teachers Institute (NTI)
National Universities Commission (NUC)
Teachers Registration Council of Nigeria (TRCN)
National Business and Technical Examinations Board (NABTEB)
Universal Basic Education Commission (UBEC)
West African Examination Council (WAEC)

Energy
Department of Petroleum Resources (DPR)
Electricity Management Services Limited (EMSL)
Energy Commission of Nigeria (ECN)
National Power Training Institute of Nigeria (NAPTIN)
Nigerian Electricity Regulatory Commission (NERC)
Nigerian National Petroleum Corporation (NNPC)
Nigerian Nuclear Regulatory Authority (NNRA)
Petroleum Product Pricing Regulatory Agency (PPPRA)
Power Holding Company of Nigeria (PHCN)
Rural Electrification Agency (REA)
Transmission Company of Nigeria (TCN)

Environment
Federal Environmental Protection Agency (FEPA)
Forestry Research Institute of Nigeria (FRIN)
National Biosafety Management Agency (NBMA)

National Environmental Standards and Regulations Enforcement Agency (NESREA)
National Oil Spill Detection and Response Agency (NOSDRA)

Health
National Health Insurance Scheme (NHIS) (www.nhis.gov.ng)
National Institute for Pharmaceutical Research and Development (NIPRD)
National Agency for the Control of AIDS (NACA)
National Agency for Food and Drug Administration and Control (NAFDAC)
National Primary Health Care Development Agency (NPHCDA)
Nigerian Institute of Medical Research (NIMR)

Professional Healthcare Regulators
Medical and Dental Council of Nigeria (MDCN)
Medical Rehabilitation Therapists Board (MRTB)
Nursing and Midwifery Council of Nigeria (NMCN)
Laboratory Scientists Council of Nigeria (LSCN)
Pharmacy Council of Nigeria (PCN)

Intelligence
Defence Intelligence Agency (DIA)
State Security Service (SSS)
National Intelligence Agency (NIA)
Cross River State Homeland Security (CRHS)

Judiciary
National Judicial Council (NJC)

Federal Judicial Service Commission (FJSC)
National Judicial Institute (NJI)

Maritime
Nigerian Maritime Administration and Safety Agency (NIMASA)
Nigerian Ports Authority (NPA)
Nigerian Shippers Council (NSC)

Media
Broadcasting Organisation of Nigeria (BON)
News Agency of Nigeria (NAN)
Nigerian Press Council (NPC)
Nigerian Television Authority (NTA)

Science and Technology
National Agency for Science and Engineering Infrastructure (NASENI)
National Biotechnology Development Agency (NABDA)
National Centre for Remote Sensing, Jos (NCRS)
National Office for Technology Acquisition and Promotion (NOTAP)
National Space Research and Development Agency (NASRDA)
Nigerian Nuclear Regulatory Authority (NNRA)
Raw Materials Research and Development Council (RMRDC)
Nigerian Communications Satellite Ltd (NIGCOMSAT)
National Centre for Technology Management (NACETEM)

Water Resources
Nigeria Hydrological Services Agency (NIHSA)
Nigerian Integrated Water Resources Commission
National Water Resources Institute (NWRI)

River Basin Development Authorities (RBDA's)

Miscellaneous
Centre for Black and African Arts and Civilization (CBAAC)
Code of Conduct Bureau (CCB)
Computer Professionals Registration Council of Nigeria (CPN)
Consumer Protection Council (CPC)
Economic and Financial Crimes Commission (EFCC)
Federal Character Commission (FCC)
Federal Housing Authority (FHA)
Independent Corrupt Practices and Other Related Offences Commission (ICPC)
Independent National Electoral Commission (INEC)
Industrial Training Fund (ITF)
Legal Aid Council of Nigeria (LACoN)
National Agency for the Prohibition of Trafficking in Persons (NAPTIP)
National Boundary Commission
National Council of Arts and Culture (NCAC)
National Economic Reconstruction Fund (NERFUND)
National Emergency Management Agency (NEMA)
National Hajj Commission of Nigeria (NaHCON) [103]
National Human Rights Commission (NHRC)
National Identity Management Commission (NIMC)
National Institute for Hospitality Tourism (NIHOTOUR)
National Lottery Regulatory Commission
National Orientation Agency (NOA)
National Poverty Eradication Programme (NAPEP)
National Salaries, Incomes and Wages Commission (NSIWC)
National Sports Commission (NSC)

Nigeria Extractive Industries Transparency Initiative (NEITI)
Nigeria Immigration Service (NIS)
Nigerian Building and Road Research Institute (NBRRI)
Nigeria Institute of Building (NIOB)
Nigerian Christian Pilgrim Commission (NCPC)
Nigerian Copyright Commission (NCC)
Nigerian Tourism Development Corporation (NTDC)
Public Complaints Commission
Surveyors Council of Nigeria

References

These references are those that may not have been documented in the main text.

http://worldpopulationreview.com

http://data.un.org/en/iso/ng.html

https://en.wikipedia.org/wiki/Demographics_of_Nigeria

https://www.iaee.org/documents/newsletterarticles/408sambo.pdf

https://www.ncc.gov.ng/stakeholder/statistics-reports/subscriber-data

http://www.doingbusiness.org/en/data/exploreeconomies/nigeria

Beyond Fears

Some other books by the same author.

Personal Injury& Clinical Negligence: Consumer Rights & Provider's Responsibilities.

About the Book..

Essentially, this book is about addressing the gaping hole in the rights of consumers: to consume goods and services that are free from harm. When an injury occurs, the consumer should and do have a right to correction and restitution. For so long, consumers of products and services have been taken for granted by manufacturers and service providers—-often with manifest abuses taking place. By focusing on clinical negligence as an example, the author used his background as a physician to illustrate the key principles that are advocated in this book. Such principles and practices include duty of care and provision of standard of care, which cut across all industrial sectors and not just in healthcare. The objective of the book is to enhance the welfare of consumers and to champion their rights. In similar manner, the author aims to raise the awareness of these rights while at the same time draw the attention of providers of goods and services to their own responsibilities. If these objectives are achieved, then, the mission of the book and the author are accomplished.

Complete Guide to Your Health

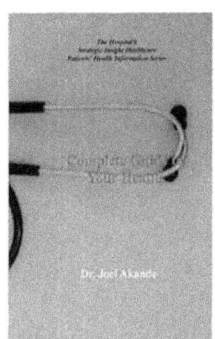

Complete Guide to Your Health is a medical compendium purposely written in plain English and devoid of complicated medical jargon. The purpose is to provide the readers with comprehensive guide to total health, emphasizing simple-to-adopt, and common sense measures to safeguard health.

Relationships: This book, tells us the stark choices, risks and benefits that lay before us in our attempt to form a relationship and even after, we have done so. You may ask: Why does a particular relationship succeed or fail? Should I befriend someone? What are the benefits of marriage?

You can order online at www.the-hospitals.com or through your reputable bookshop.

www.ingramcontent.com/pod-product-compliance
Lightning Source LLC
LaVergne TN
LVHW021352080426
835508LV00020B/2251